Improving the Use of
Social Studies Textbooks

William E. Patton, Editor

National Council for the Social Studies • Bulletin 63

ABOUT THE EDITOR

William E. Patton taught in public schools in the state of Washington for ten years. He received his Master's degree and his Doctorate from the University of Washington. He is currently a member of the faculty in the Graduate School of Education at Kent State University, Ohio, where he has teaching responsibilities in the Department of Elementary Education and in the Department of Curriculum and Instruction.

Library of Congress Catalog Card Number: 08-91160
ISBN 0-87986-027-8
Copyright © 1980 by the
NATIONAL COUNCIL FOR THE SOCIAL STUDIES
3615 Wisconsin Ave., N.W., Washington, D.C. 20016

Foreword

The first history teacher I really liked turned our textbook into a resource of some interest by creating nonsense games out of the questions at the end of the chapter, with crazy, hilarious, and absurd consequences. We students loved it! As a result I did well in history. I don't remember the textbook but do know that the teacher's system of using it *in a special way* helped me. This Bulletin is intended to help teachers in the same, if somewhat more sober, way.

As we are well aware, studies show that textbooks remain the school's most widely used curriculum tool. Although a text can meet the general need very well, at times all of us wish such books could do everything. Unfortunately, they cannot. In fact, texts can easily become outdated, can contribute to destructive stereotyping of women and ethnic groups, and can fail to meet the needs of the curriculum in many other ways.

Teachers are expected to use textbooks as effective learning tools no matter what the books' inadequacies may be. Unfortunately, as a result of all the other demands on teachers' time, few hours remain to plan and implement a First Aid program for a deficient textbook. This Bulletin is intended to help teachers deal with that problem. Its publication is another illustration of the concern of the National Council for the Social Studies for the needs of classroom teachers, who make up the largest percentage of the membership of our organization. It is our hope that this book will prove to be a useful tool in helping provide high quality instruction for students everywhere.

By focusing on lessons and exercises which can be used with students, this Bulletin goes beyond simply giving teachers advice, and it makes it possible for them to move directly from the Bulletin to the classroom. Such an approach should make this a very popular way of giving textbooks that additional something they all need.

Todd Clark, *President*
National Council for the Social Studies

Preface

"Nothing is inevitable except death and taxes" goes an old saying. There are teachers today who would add "textbooks" to the list.

Certainly, there is proof to demonstrate the widespread use of textbooks throughout the United States. The preeminence of the textbook was documented in a study conducted by John Goodlad and his associates. Sixty-seven schools in the United States were examined, and the following conclusion was reached:

> The curriculum framework for most of the schools in our sample was supplied, as far as we were able to determine, by guides prepared at local, county, and state levels. These and textbooks provided the major sources of the schools' curricula. . . .[1]

Shaver, Davis, and Helburn also pointed out that, within the context of the social studies classroom, textbooks continue to be the dominant instructional tool.[2] Then, in 1980, Project SPAN, a major study conducted by the Social Science Education Consortium and sponsored by the National Science Foundation, reported:

The findings of recent research studies emphatically point out that certain curriculum materials, *especially commercially published textbooks*, are the central tool for teaching social studies. . . . The picture of curriculum materials which emerges from the data is that materials, *particularly texts*, are extensively used.[3]

Faced with the fact that textbooks play a dominant role in the classroom, one may react in at least two ways: (1) to lament the use of textbooks and insist that they be discarded at once, or (2) to accept the reality of the situation and do everything possible to improve the ways in which textbooks are used. This Bulletin takes the second course.

Thus, this book is designed to show how it is possible to update the dated, strengthen reading comprehension, study pictures, correct ethnic and sex stereotypes, and evaluate the strengths and weaknesses of today's textbooks. A special bibliography is provided to encourage additional study and research.

Too many critics of textbooks seem to be willing to stop their work with the identification of shortcomings. They apply their criteria to textbooks, announce the results dramatically, and move on to new targets. What they fail to do is to *correct* deficiencies in the books.

One technique employed in several chapters in this Bulletin for making such corrections is called *Springboard Lessons*. A specific problem is the starting point—or springboard—for developing ways of utilizing a textbook in a more effective manner.

---

[1]J. I. Goodlad, M. F. Klein, and Associates, *Looking Behind the Classroom Door* (Worthington, Ohio: Jones, 1974), p. 41.

[2]J. P. Shaver, O. L. Davis, Jr., and S. W. Helburn, "The Status of Social Studies Education: Implications from Three NSF Studies," *Social Education* (February 1979), p. 151.

[3]D. P. Superka, S. Hawke, and I. Morrissett, "The Current and Future Status of the Social Studies," *Social Education* (May 1980), pp. 365–366. Italics mine.

Each Springboard Lesson will answer four questions: What is the nature of the problem in the textbook? What purpose will be accomplished by its solution or correction? How will the solution or correction be carried out with the students? Where can additional information be found to help in planning and implementing the lesson?

Those chapters that do not contain Springboard Lessons will feature other exercises and techniques that can be used to improve the use of social studies textbooks. This has been done to make this Bulletin as practical as possible for classroom use.

I am grateful to Donald O. Schneider, Mary Jo McGee Brown, Thomas N. Turner, Martin W. Sandler, and Jean Dresden Grambs for their valuable contributions to this publication. A special salute goes to those dedicated social studies teachers who, in the long run, will be responsible for the successful execution of the ideas presented in this book.

William E. Patton, *Editor*

Acknowledgments

Chapter 2, "Helping Students Study and Understand Their Social Studies Textbooks," is reprinted from *Social Education*, February 1980.

Chapter 3, "Making the Social Studies Textbook a More Effective Tool for Less Able Readers," is reprinted from *Social Education*, January 1976.

Chapter 4, "How To Read Pictures," is abridged and adapted from *In Search of America, Annotated Edition* by Martin W. Sandler, © Copyright, 1975, by Ginn and Company (Xerox Corporation). Used with permission.

Contents

Chapter 1

Updating the Outdated in Textbooks

William E. Patton

One frustration experienced by authors and publishers of social studies textbooks results from the realization that some parts of their publications will be outdated when they reach the classroom. Social studies textbooks available today, unlike most of those published during earlier periods, are able to meet a number of needs of teachers. Realistic readability levels, clearly developed concepts, discussions of values, and other desirable features are present in recently published textbooks. The reality remains, however, that many parts of textbooks either are outdated or will be outdated before the instructional life of the material has expired.

Aspects of social studies textbooks which are susceptible to being outmoded are numerous. The names of contemporary leaders of nations, maps with political boundaries and names, charts with data re-

WILLIAM E. PATTON is a faculty member in the Graduate School of Education, Kent State University, Ohio.

flecting specific years, and references to current international relations are a few examples. In the midst of a world which is characterized by change, the burden for being responsive to new conditions and information thus comes back to the social studies teacher. The teacher who has an array of techniques for updating the outdated does not need to feel frustration with social studies textbooks.

UPDATING TECHNIQUES

The term "technique" will be used in this chapter to convey the importance of using systematic procedures to correct outdated parts of textbooks. When a teacher employs specific techniques to correct the visual and verbal elements of printed material, the practice can become a strategy if it is conducted over time. Used once or twice, it is a technique; used several times it becomes a tactic; finally, continuous use results in it developing into a strategy. The last practice is stressed in this section. Procedures are described to help teachers make corrective techniques a continuous function—that is, a strategy.

Updating techniques will be examined in three areas. The first two focus on the gathering and use of new visuals and information. The third discusses techniques for using the outdated features of textbooks, particularly in discontinued adoptions. The furnaces in textbook depositories, unfortunately, have short-circuited many exciting possibilities for the use of outdated social studies textbooks.

Updating with Visuals

The word "visual" is used here to represent photographs, paintings, illustrations, cartoons, maps, graphs, and charts. The first step in being able to use them for corrective purposes is finding examples. Leonard Kenworthy has identified more than ten different sources for pictures, ranging from Embassies and Information Services to study prints.[1] If an enterprising teacher has not already tapped the local newspaper office, it is worth noting that visuals from cartoons to graphs can be obtained there. Press photographers and the wire services provide newspapers with more visuals than they ever use on a daily basis. Sometimes teachers may gain access to some of these materials.

Magazines have always been a popular source of visuals. One secret to success is knowing which magazines have items that social studies teachers need. *Atlas World Press Review*, for example, publishes political cartoons from newspapers representing many countries in the world. *Fortune* has outstanding charts and graphs with current and projected economic information. Magazines such as *Newsweek* and *Time* have pictures of current events and personalities, as well as a large assortment of graphs and charts. Credit-card holders, because of services purchased from some major oil companies, often receive magazines which have excellent maps. Public libraries, of course, are good places to browse to identify magazines that meet special needs. While in the library, teachers can ask the periodical librarian about extra back issues. As a result of one casual request, one fortunate teacher received a set of *National Geographic* covering a period from the 1920s through the 1950s.

The second step in working to update outdated textbook material is organizing visuals. A teacher's file of visuals is invaluable. Initially, a file could be organized by type of visual, such as cartoons, charts, and current personalities. After a period of time, particularly if more than one teacher is gathering visuals, types may have to be subdivided by topic. Cartoons may be subdivided into topics such as political (local, national, and international) and social (entertainment, family relations, and hunger). Some form of lamination should be employed to preserve visuals. Of course, a picture file can have a number of uses, in addition to correcting outdated visuals. John Michaelis reviews different uses, which include introducing units and heightening critical thinking.[2]

The next step in correcting outdated visuals in textbooks is the actual use of the new material. Teacher- and student-made bulletin boards offer many possibilities. Pictures of new leaders who have replaced those shown in textbooks could be displayed with their predecessors. A map of the United States or of the world could be placed at the center of the board. Pins and yarn could connect the two pictures with one location. Mayors Daley and Byrne in Chicago and Prime Ministers Heath and Thatcher in London are examples of pictures that could be displayed. The bulletin board's title might be "Changing Faces" or "Ins and Outs of Leaders."

A common problem among curricular materials at all levels is the stereotyping of Third World countries and their levels of social, economic, and political development. Some textbooks have not developed images of Third World nations that deviate significantly from Olney's description of the state of society in the Persian world during the first half of the nineteenth century.

---

[1] L. S. Kenworthy, *Reach for a Picture* (Washington, D.C.: National Council for the Social Studies, 1977), pp. 5–6.

[2] J. U. Michaelis, *Social Studies for Children in a Democracy* (Englewood Cliffs, N.J.: Prentice-Hall, 1976), pp. 392–394.

In the *half-civilized state*, men subsist by agriculture and pasturage, and understand many of the arts; but science, literature, and foreign commerce are almost unknown. They have established laws and religion, and some of their finer manufactures they have carried to a high degree of perfection. The most noted in this state of society are the Persians.[3]

The lack of political stability in many Latin American countries does not mean that each country is totally rural and agrarian. The tribalism in Nigeria and Afghanistan has not reduced the significant cultural achievements of these nations. Incorrect images of these countries come from a variety of sources. Textbooks may contribute only to the extent that they cannot do exhaustive pictorial essays on every country in the world. Also, the basis for comparison is usually the more technologically advanced countries of Europe and North America. Graphs and charts typically depict Third World countries as being "below" the advanced nations in an economic or technological way. Learning centers can be developed for primary and middle-school students that deal with advancements in Third World countries. One set of study activities could picture architectural contributions in urban centers of the Third World. A second set might focus on past and current scientific contributions from Third World countries. Secondary students could use pictures of places, persons, and artifacts that trace the roots of greatness that are the heritage of many Third World countries. The new visuals could contribute to correcting stereotypes of Third World countries.

Another use of visuals to update information in social studies textbooks relates to the technological innovations sweeping the electronics industry. Micro-circuitry, liquid crystals, and replaceable components are recent developments. Students have daily contact with many results of the new technology in toys, kitchen appliances, cars, watches, and calculators. Some textbooks have not incorporated information about

---

[3]J. Olney, *A Practical System of Modern Geography; or a View of the World* (New York: Pratt, Woodford & Company, 1850), p. 51.

the newer technologies in relevant chapters. Advertisement brochures, catalogues, and magazines such as *Popular Mechanics* are excellent sources for visuals. Students can prepare pictorial timelines, participate in mini-science fairs, and print classroom science bulletins in conjunction with social studies activities to update technological innovations.

Updating with Information

The sections on visuals and information have been separated in this chapter. Many times, however, the social studies teacher will use both types of updating techniques simultaneously. A new graph from a magazine and updated information from an almanac can be used with one updating technique. Information, in this context, refers to quantitative data. For example, secondary textbooks depend on census data for many factual and conceptual elements. 1970 census data are unreliable for many new purposes with the passing of the decade, and the results of the 1980 census will not be available in textbooks for classroom use for some time. However, updated census data can be obtained from county and municipal planning departments and from projections made by the federal government that are based on samples from around the United States. These new data can be used in several ways: (1) calculating revenue-sharing income for local governments, (2) computing per capita income figures based on GNP, and (3) documenting white flight on one hand and urban buildup on the other. Census data in most textbooks are often too outdated to be useful except as a springboard to other learning.

United States history textbooks used by students at the fifth-grade level may deal with the number of eligible voters who actually cast ballots during each presidential election. The pattern across the elections from 1960 to 1976 reflects a decrease in the percentage of eligible voters casting ballots. The textbooks may not have the 1976 figures, and those for 1980 are not a reality as of this writing. The students could formulate hypotheses regarding the voting patterns between 1960 and 1972. Updated information from the 1976 election could be obtained. (After November of 1980, a second set of data will be available.) The new information would make it possible for the students to test their hypotheses and draw conclusions that go beyond information in their current social studies textbooks.

Elementary textbooks rarely use specific prices of food and clothing as part of the narrative. Visuals may have some reference to prices. An excellent way to teach the concept of inflation and update information about prices given in textbooks is to organize price timelines for periods between three and nine months. In addition to creating high interest, this constant updating technique has high visibility as a social studies activity. Once a week a student or small group of students would have the responsibility for checking the local newspaper for prices. New prices would be entered on the timeline. Students would need to know that most prices in newspapers are sale prices. They could shop with parents, travel to gas stations, and check clothing stores. At set intervals the students could calculate inflation rates and compare them to those announced by the federal government each month. The latter step might be modified for lower elementary students because of limitations in their computation skills.

An information file can be organized in a manner similar to a file for visuals. The updated information might fit into categories such as population, taxes, prices, and interest rates. A teacher may want to put a bar graph in the visual file and in the information file. It could serve two different purposes.

Using the Outdated

The two previous sections stressed the importance of going beyond the outdated by gathering and using updated visuals and information. The basic assumption underlying the discussion in this section is the value of outdated materials for accomplishing purposes other than those for which they were originally intended. The techniques for using the outdated are keyed to the belief that nothing in the hands of creative social studies teachers is outdated. A political

cartoon of Theodore Roosevelt may fail to serve a useful purpose on page 347 of a social studies textbook copyrighted in 1958. However, twenty-eight copies of the same cartoon that have been laminated and placed in the hands of high school students may be the first step in an exciting lesson in United States history.

Political cartoons from outdated textbooks can be used in a number of ways. Four different political cartoons from as many different textbooks depicting Theodore Roosevelt could be used to develop generalizations or hypotheses by secondary students. As an activity started during the first day of a unit on Roosevelt or the Progressive Era, there could be testing of the generalization or hypothesis with new information gained throughout subsequent lessons. Middle-school students might use a set of laminated political cartoons to identify major symbols for citizens of the United States and for American social, economic, and political life. This could be one of several techniques used by teachers to develop the skill of interpreting political cartoons.

Graphs from social studies textbooks are also useful for developing interpretation skills. A resource file of graphs related to geography (temperature, rainfall), economics (income, inflation), and other social sciences could be prepared. The individual graphs could be filed according to the level of skill needed to read the graph and interpret its message. The graphs might be organized as a learning center for primary or middle-school students. Secondary pupils might use a similar resource file system. This time, however, the teacher would have one or two conclusions for each graph. The student would have the task of determining the validity of each conclusion. A rationale might be written to support its status as a valid conclusion, as an invalid conclusion, or as insufficient information to make a judgment. Students themselves can write conclusions and work in small groups to determine their validity.

The pictures that fill social studies textbooks are a wasted resource when they are ignored. A file on families of the world for use in multicultural education is an important source to supplement pictures in an outdated textbook. A similar file could be established for the various racial and ethnic groups in the United States. A collection of stereotyped roles for women and men can be gathered. Sets of pictures of men and women in nonstereotypic roles, which are more difficult to find in books with older copyrights, can be prepared. Pictures for bulletin boards on countries of the world could be available in outdated material. Timelines of scientific advancements or fashions could be constructed from these pictures. Collages with different levels of conceptual difficulty could be designed. At the elementary level, pictures to form a collage depicting time could be shown. A more complex collage pattern for secondary students could be constructed to demonstrate the concept of regionalism. The collage is an excellent focus for an inquiry/discovery lesson. Students could also construct collages from old textbooks to express concepts and generalizations as well as values.

Even sections of narrative can be used from outdated textbooks. Some social studies textbooks have in-depth discussions of specific individuals. These could be cut out and placed in a file or used to make books of reading for students on specific topics, such as women in United States history and the American Presidency. Parts of a narrative with high interest value for middle-school and secondary students could be used on cards to teach social studies, reading skills, or reading in the content area. Examples of sexist narrative could be used to teach students to write nonsexist essays in social studies. Technical words from the social sciences could be posted on cards and used for vocabulary-building activities with elementary students.

When a school system is adopting new social studies textbooks, teachers should join together and make a case to keep the old books for other purposes. The material that an elementary school faculty could glean from an entire series is staggering. One set of old government textbooks in a high school also would produce dozens of useable items. A group of teachers could have a brainstorming session on how to use the outdated books. These teachers could generate an excellent list of uses in a short period of time. Labeling a textbook "outdated" may reduce its value to some people, but social studies teachers should see it as an unexpected windfall.

SPRINGBOARD LESSONS

Many different techniques for the identification, organization, and use of outdated aspects of social studies textbooks have been mentioned in this chapter. The process of using these techniques over time results in an important strategy for teachers' decision-making. Updating the outdated does not happen by chance, however. The problem must be identified, visuals and/or information must be gathered to update, and an activity at the appropriate grade level must be devised to implement the correction. (**Springboard Lessons appear on pp. 6−8.**)

Springboard Lesson 1 outlines activities for students that accomplish two purposes. First, students learn to read visuals critically. Second, the demands for metrication can be met in the social studies classroom. The elementary students are involved in activities that use everyday aspects of metric measures. These activities are implemented to update the outdated aspects of visuals in elementary social studies textbooks.

SPRINGBOARD LESSON 1

Elementary—Updating with Visuals

Description:

Many publishers of social studies textbooks have successfully converted to the metric system where instances of weights and measures are used. This is not true in all situations. Some elementary textbooks have maps and graphs with measures in miles and the Fahrenheit scale. Pictures of grocery and hardware products are clearly visible with weights and measures in ounces, pounds, and pints. The narrative makes no reference to any figures that would need conversion to the metric system. The updating process would be instituted to meet the needs of metrication.

Objective:

The students will convert length, area, volume or capacity, and weight units into metric equivalents.

Activities:

1. The students would be placed in small work teams (3 or 4 in each team). A chapter in the textbook would be given to each team. Its first task would involve the careful examination of all visual items in the textbook. The nature of the weight or measure and its location would be written on a 3″ by 5″ card for each item. Once the teams have reported back to the class on their findings, the conversion activity can begin. A supplementary book or pamphlet could be given to any team that did not have examples in its chapter. With graphs the students would construct new examples and place divisions for U.S. customary units and metric units; e.g., F and C on a temperature graph. Pictures from a file or magazine could be glued to backing paper to match the products shown in the textbook. The new weight or measure would be placed on a label below the picture. An integrated lesson with mathematics would help the students do the conversions.
2. The teacher could organize a team Metric Bee or a Team Challenge activity to work with the converted weights and measures. Using the pictures and graphs developed by the children or outdated pictures cut from old textbooks, the teacher could give the U.S. customary unit figures, and students would have 8 to 12 seconds to come up with the metric equivalent. Sample cards: 20° F, 36 ounces, and 2 acres.

Information Sources:

Michaelis, J. U. *Social Studies for Children in a Democracy* (6th Ed.). Englewood Cliffs, N.J.: Prentice-Hall, 1976, pp. 345–346.

Whitman, N. C., and Braun, F. G. *The Metric System: A Laboratory Approach for Teachers*. New York: Wiley & Sons, 1978.

Springboard Lesson 2 involves inter-mediate/middle-school students in active learning experiences. One allows them to "destroy" a textbook while engaged in positive instruction. The students are using outdated textbooks to satisfy their needs for high-interest, fast-paced activities. The springboard also illustrates how students with different skill levels can be involved in aspects of updating activities.

SPRINGBOARD LESSON 2

Intermediate/Middle School—Using the Outdated

Description:

Students in upper elementary and lower junior high grades are often interested in change, variety, and alternatives. Skills of analysis through establishing conceptual relationships and comparing and contrasting are a natural outcome of their interest. The organization of most social studies textbooks follows a regional or chronological format at the intermediate/middle-school level. To trace a thematic change in industrial or agricultural methods, transportation, and social developments, a student must persevere for an entire school year. The outmoded social studies textbooks offer a vehicle for maximizing students' interest in change and variety. The visuals and narrative can be reorganized to deliver single lessons or three-to-four-lesson units on a variety of appropriate thematic topics. These topics might include agricultural techniques, the evolution of transportation, and significant personalities.

Objective:

The students will display their comprehension of thematic elements in social studies by developing visual and written essays.

Activities:

1. Working individually or in small groups, students would be given a paragraph representing an unfinished story. These stories would be thematic starters developed by the teacher or an above-average student. Each student or group would complete the story with visuals from obsolete textbooks. The finished stories could be presented orally to the class, or a written narrative might accompany the visuals.
2. The teacher could develop thematic timelines on a variety of topics. Fashions, wars, and architecture might be used. Each visual from an outdated textbook would be placed on a separate card. The timelines would form packets of cards which could be stored in envelopes. These packets could be used with slower learners to develop different concepts, or they might be free-time activities for all students.
3. Older students could identify a theme such as working conditions in the United States and develop an in-depth study using visuals (pictures and graphs) from discarded textbooks to communicate the evolution of working conditions.

Information Source:

Jarolimek, J. *Social Studies in Elementary Education* (5th Edition). New York: Macmillan, 1977, pp. 194–201.

Springboard Lesson 3 shows why new information needs to be gathered in secondary classrooms to make contemporary topics meaningful. Updated information is needed for decision-making about real issues. Higher level cognitive activities are encouraged with the procedures. Important affective learning experiences could be integrated with the second activity because one form of updated information gathered is qualitative.

SPRINGBOARD LESSON 3

Secondary—Updating with Information

Description:

Secondary social studies textbooks used in areas such as United States history and contemporary problems have a difficulty concerning the outdating of information used to describe recent local, national, and international situations. What textbook published in 1978 would have graphs reflecting the spiraling costs of precious metals such as silver, gold, and platinum? How accurate are the figures concerning oil prices set and reset by members of the oil-producing nations' pricing cartel—OPEC? The examples are numerous. The reality of today's world is rapid change. The results of changes cannot be in all textbooks used in every secondary social studies classroom. The use of supplementary materials can help to correct the information lag. Cost, however, may make this difficult.

Objective:

The students will update information on contemporary issues by identifying information deficiencies and by gathering new information.

Activities:

1. Larger numbers of women are entering the labor force in the United States. In discussing the trend, a teacher might refer students to figures in the textbook from the Department of Labor regarding workers and income by sex. The teacher would write the following statement on the chalkboard: "As the number of female workers increased in relation to the number of male workers during the 1970s, the gap between the salaries of women and men *increased*." The students would seek new information to test the teacher's hypothesis. (It is valid for occupations from service industries to that of college professors.)

2. Wars are costly! The full impact in terms of economic and social costs of the Vietnam War has not been included in many secondary textbooks. Some still have the United States military in South Viet Nam. Information of a quantitative nature (military spending, lost lives) and qualitative nature (social consequences for the United States and South Viet Nam resulting from the war) would be gathered. Narrative, charts, and graphs could be prepared by the students and compared to similar information on World War II. Financial figures would need to be adjusted to compare the 1940s and 1970s.

Information Source:

Lewis, D. K. "A Response to Inequality: Black Women, Racism, and Sexism." *Signs: Journal of Women in Culture and Society*, Winter 1977, 3, pp. 339–361.

Chapter 2

Helping Students Study and Understand Their Social Studies Textbooks

Donald O. Schneider and Mary Jo McGee Brown

"I like that textbook, it's got substance, but I'll have to use a watered-down text that my students can read . . . ."

"This is ridiculous! They expect me to use a textbook that must be written two or three grade levels above the capabilities of most of my students."

Sound familiar? If you haven't expressed views similar to these, you no doubt have heard them expressed by others. Many social studies teachers, most of whom have had little training in the formal aspects of teaching reading, find themselves searching for ways of coming to grips with the "reading problem." The purpose of this chapter is to suggest a strategy and illus-trate briefly some activities that can aid students' comprehension of content and foster development of their skills to read and use their textbooks.

DEVELOPING AN INSTRUCTIONAL STRATEGY

As with any other aspect of teaching, the development of an instructional strategy for helping students make effective use of their textbooks is likely to pay dividends in learning outcomes.[1] Essentially such a strategy should incorporate three phases: (1) a pre-reading phase for assessing skills, diagnosing needs, and motivating students for subsequent instruction; (2) the reading

---

DONALD O. SCHNEIDER is Associate Professor of Social Science Education at the University of Georgia.

MARY JO McGEE BROWN is a recent doctoral graduate from the Social Science Education Department at the University of Georgia.

[1]Although the research is mixed, positive gains have been reported in several studies, some of which are included in the three reports published by the Reading and Language Arts Center of Syracuse University, edited by Harold Herber and others, *Research in Reading in the Content Areas*, 1969, 1973, 1977.

phase for guiding students to search out desired information and intellectually interact with and comprehend the message; and (3) the post-reading phase for reinforcing learning, reflection on the meaning and possible use of the newly acquired knowledge. Figure 1, on p. 11, lists some alternatives to be considered in developing a strategy. Some of the suggested activities may be switched from one phase to another, depending on the overall strategy. For example, a vocabulary exercise may be used in the pre-reading phase, or a categorization task could be used after the reading assignment and related discussion have been completed. The point is that a logical, coherent set of before, during, and after activities be planned as part of an overall instructional strategy.

1. Pre-Reading Phase

Textbook Introduction

Although this inspectional reading activity is generally used only at the beginning of a school term, it can be a valuable assessment, diagnostic, and teaching device. Too often we erroneously assume that our students know how to use a textbook so that they can quickly and easily locate specific information. Introduction exercises can be designed to have students: (1) identify the authors and their professional positions, the title and general content of the text, the number of units and chapters, and the publication date; (2) use the table of contents, listings of maps, graphs or other illustrations, index, glossary, and appendix in order to locate specific information in the text; and (3) skim or scan sections of the text to determine the pattern of organization (Is there a topic sentence at the beginning of the passage or paragraph; does it come at the end; or does it have one at all?); how headings, special symbols, and italicized print may be used as clues in reading (What is the significance of different type size, print, color, and headings?); the specific use of photographs and graphic illustrations, including captions; and how special study aids, such as pre-reading and review questions, lists of terms, and other devices, may help in comprehension. Figure 2, on p. 12, provides an illustration of a textbook introduction exercise.

Structured Overviews

A structured overview is a graphic and hierarchical presentation of the relationships of key ideas and concepts to be encountered in the reading and subsequent instructional activities.[2] It is a kind of cognitive map that is used prior to the systematic study phase to help students relate new ideas and information to previously learned relevant concepts. It can also be used to help students relate the structure of the new unit to the overall context of the course. Figure 3, on p. 12, is an example of a structured overview for a rather typical section of a history textbook.

Both you and your students become involved in creating and using the structured overview. After reading the textbook unit or chapter, you create an initial version to help clarify your instructional objectives and as a guide for planning. Select the major ideas, concepts, terms, and appropriate illustrations from the reading. Arrange these graphically to show their relationships to one another. Conceptual elements such as category, attributes, examples, action, agents of action, object or recipient of action, purpose, cause, location, and quality of event or action may be shown. You may present your scheme to students directly, or you may choose to lead students to create their own simple scheme through a word association brainstorming session with the key concept or term from the reading (e.g., federalism, revolution, pollution, money, etc.). Initially, the structured overview should be simple. As study progresses, you and the students can add to it and rearrange it. Display the scheme on a bulletin board, chalkboard, or overhead projector. Discuss it. Have students define concepts, explain relationships, and justify any reorganization. In short, use it as a dynamic scheme open to amplification and change.

---

[2]Richard F. Barron, "The Use of Vocabulary as an Advance Organizer," in *Research in Reading in the Content Areas*, eds., Harold Herber and Peter L. Sanders (Syracuse, New York: Syracuse University Reading and Language Arts Center, 1969), pp. 29–39.

**Figure 1. Developing an Instructional Strategy for
Guiding Students' Reading in the Social Studies: Some Alternatives**

1. Pre-Reading Phase: Assessing, Diagnosing, and Setting the Stage
   A. Pretest, Informal Reading Test, Attitude Inventory
   B. Structured Overview, Semantic Map, Advance Organizer
   C. Role Playing; Simulation Games
   D. Provocative Audio, Visual, or Other Experiences
   E. Inspectional Reading (skimming or scanning)
   F. Cloze Tasks (filling in missing words from passage)
   G. Word Association Activities

2. Reading Phase: Guiding Reading, Interaction, and Comprehension
   A. "Informal" Teacher Questions
   B. Textbook Study Questions
   C. Reading Guides
      (1) Level Guide, Single or Multi-Level Guide
      (2) Pattern Guide
      (3) Concept Guide
      (4) Reaction Guide
      (5) Selective Reading/Process Guide
   D. Other Guiding Procedures
      (1) SQ3R—Survey, Question, Read, Recite, and Review
      (2) Guided Reading Procedure (Manzo)

3. Post-Reading Phase: Providing for Reinforcement, Reflection, and
   Application
   A. Reflective Discussion
      (1) Class Discussion of Reading Guide Responses
      (2) Compare/Contrast Pre-Reading Activity with Guide Responses
      (3) Reconsideration of Structured Overview
   B. Concept and Vocabulary Development Activities
      (1) Word Recognition Exercises: Word Hunts, Cryptograms
      (2) Meaning Exercises: Word Puzzles, Matching, Categorization,
          Word Association
      (3) Context Meaning Activities: Cloze Procedure, Word Studies
          (root words, multiple meaning words, prefixes, suffixes)
   C. Application/Extension Activities
      (1) Simulation Game, Panel Discussion, Guest Speaker, Field Expe-
          riences, Individual Research and Reports, etc.
      (2) Post-Test (pre-test or new and more comprehensive assessment)
      (3) Begin Pre-Reading Phase on New Correlated "Unit" of Study,
          Providing Transitions and Showing Relationships.

Figure 2. Textbook Introduction for *Magruder's American Government*[3]

---

1. Frank A. Magruder is the original author of this textbook. Who has made the present revisions and what indication do you have that he or she is qualified to do this?

(Purpose: Author identification and credibility of information in text.)

2. How current is the information in this book?

(Purpose: Identification of copyright date.)

3. Which of the following persons has the most written about him in this book: Oliver Ellsworth, John Jay, Martin Luther King, Jr., Abraham Lincoln?

(Purpose: Use of index.)

4. What method of relating information is used on pages 341, 372, 389, 421, and 432?

(Purpose: Use of graphics.)

5. Can you find the page number of the Declaration of Independence in the Table of Contents? What page is it on?

(Purpose: Use of Table of Contents)

6. On what page will you find a case study on "Attitudes Toward Taxation"? How is this section different from the rest of the chapter?

(Purpose: Use of Table of Contents and understanding text organization.)

7. Look through Chapter 6 very quickly. If you wanted to get a quick idea of its content, what page would you turn to?

(Purpose: To identify chapter organization and special study devices.)

Figure 3. Structured Overview for *Rise of the American Nation*, Unit 5 and Chapter 18[4]

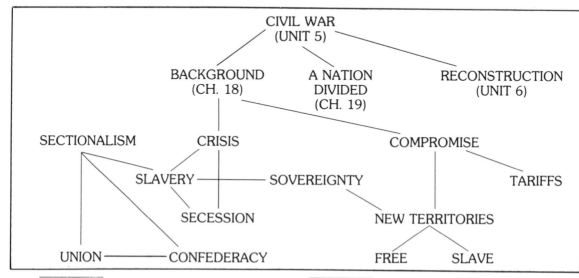

---

[3]William A. McClenaghan, *Magruder's American Government* (Boston: Allyn and Bacon, 1977).

[4]Lewis Paul Todd and Merle Curti, *Rise of the American Nation*, Heritage ed. (New York: Harcourt Brace Jovanovich, 1977).

2. The Reading Phase: Study Guides

Study guides for reading are certainly not a new form of instructional device. But in recent years more systematic development and research have been undertaken, and social studies teachers now have at their disposal several different types of guides to accomplish different purposes. Among these are levels of comprehension guides, concept guides, pattern guides, selective process guides, listening guides, viewing guides, and reaction guides. The first four lend themselves especially well to use with social studies textbooks.

Before elaborating on these individual forms of guides, however, some basic guidelines and cautions about the use of guides are in order. First, do not use guides with every reading assignment. Consider using a guide at the beginning of the year to serve as a model to students for the textbook reading process. Subsequently, use guides for difficult sections of the text or with students who need special help. Vary the form of the guide. Instructional variety reduces boredom and increases motivation. Do not grade students' work on guides or use them as tests. They are most effective when used as springboards for discussion. In fact, discussion among pairs or groups of students and total classes is essential. Guides should not be used only as individual class or homework assignments. Otherwise they may deteriorate into meaningless "busywork." In general, guides are most effective when created to accomplish specific purposes with a particular text, taking into consideration the level of reading proficiency of a specific group of students.[5]

Level Guide

Guides of this type are constructed on the premise that reading comprehension takes place at three different intellectual levels. Briefly, these three levels are: (1) literal, or what the author specifically states; (2) inferential, or what the author means by what he says; and (3) application, or how the information can be used. Such guides may be constructed using either questions or statements. A widely advocated form of this type of guide is the Three Level Guide developed by Harold Herber.[6] Students are asked to select statements that they think apply to the passage. For example, suppose the students have read a passage on the Boston Tea Party in Henry Graff's *The Free and the Brave*.[7] The following would tap students' comprehension at each level.

Literal: Mohawk Indians dumped the tea. The Tea Party took place in Boston Harbor.

Interpretive: Many American Colonists were willing to support action—even illegal action—against the King's power.

Applied: Governments should take steps to enforce the laws or people won't obey them.

As is readily apparent, the two higher level statements are likely to stimulate much discussion, and that is precisely one of the purposes of the guide. (For further illustration and elaboration on how to construct the guide, see Ronald J. Hash and Mollie B. Bailey, "A Classroom Strategy: Improving Social Studies Comprehension," *Social Education* 42 [January, 1978], pp. 24–26.)

Whether you use the Herber model or some other, we would like to emphasize that a major purpose for using this form of guide should be to help students learn to extend their comprehension from the literal to the applied level. For some students it may seem desirable to use only a literal level guide because "They've got to know the facts first!" But literal level comprehension is insufficient. Students need opportunities and guidance to develop both reading and thinking processes that will help them get more out of their textbook reading, so include at least some questions at the more sophisticated levels for all students.

[5]Adapted from Thomas H. Estes and Joseph L. Vaughan, Jr., *Reading and Learning in the Content Classroom* (Boston: Allyn and Bacon, 1978), p. 156.

[6]Harold L. Herber, *Teaching Reading in Content Areas* (Englewood Cliffs, New Jersey: Prentice-Hall, Inc., 1970).

[7]Henry F. Graff, *The Free and the Brave*, 3rd edition (Chicago: Rand McNally, 1977).

Pattern Guide

Virtually all authors organize their texts according to some overall organizational pattern. Chronological organization is a typical pattern in history texts. Geography texts frequently use a regional/spatial pattern. Recognizing the overall pattern is obviously important. This can be a focal point in course and textbook introductions. Also important, however, are the numerous sub-patterns used within chapters, or even paragraphs. Some typical patterns found in social studies texts are (1) sequence or time order, (2) listing, (3) comparison and contrast, and (4) cause and effect. Frequently, authors cue the reader about the pattern through the use of signal words. Figure 4, on p. 15, provides a partial list of these signal words as identified by Vacca under each of the four categories. By having students become more alert to the use and significance of these signal words, students will be more likely to comprehend the main idea and supporting details of the passage. An illustration of comparison-contrast pattern guide that results in a data retrieval chart is found in Figure 5, on p. 15.

Concept Guide

The purpose of a concept guide is to help students learn concepts through categorization and association. Some texts include a heavy amount of conceptual material, and concept guides may serve a useful function in breaking down the learning task into logical components. Guides of this type typically consist of two parts. The first part focuses on the concept labels, definitions, criteria, or elements. The second part provides categorization, association, and differentiation tasks with appropriate examples. An example of these two elements of concept development can be found in Figure 6, I.1. and III on pp. 16–17. (See also C. Glennon Rowell, "Vocabulary Development in the Social Studies," *Social Education 42* [January, 1978] pp. 11–12.)

Selective Reading Process Guide

Reading process guides serve to lead students through a reading assignment sometimes page by page or even paragraph by paragraph, emphasizing organizational patterns, key ideas, concepts, details, liter-

al meaning, or possible applications, while at the same time focusing on the process and skills of reading. They may incorporate elements of all other types of guides, but they differ in that they actually suggest *how* the student should go about reading the assignment. For example, in one form of a process guide—the Guide-O-Rama—the teacher tells students to "skim page 56 looking for . . .; scan the section on . . .; skip over to page. . . ." It is as though the teacher were tutoring or guiding the students as they read their texts.[8]

To construct such a guide you need to decide on your objectives for the reading very specifically, identifying the major ideas, concepts, details, and other information you wish to emphasize. This may mean that you will have students skip various pages or sections or only skim them (thus encouraging them to vary their reading rate according to the purpose). Once you have decided what you want to emphasize and what to eliminate or treat lightly, prepare the written guide as though it were a form of road map. State exactly what and where to read, what to look for, and what to do with it when found. Provide appropriate cues and opportunities for responses such as "Skip this section . . . Read this section with care! The main idea is in this paragraph . . . Skim these pages . . . Read to find 3 examples of . . . and write them here . . . Turn back to page 36. How does it relate to this chapter?" Hallmarks of this type of guide are its specificity, directiveness, informality, and even its humor. Don't be afraid to add a witty line, a pun, or other humorous reference from time to time. Figure 6, on pp. 16–17, is an excerpt from a "Guide-O-Rama."

Some teachers object to this type of guided reading because they view it as "spoon feeding." Indeed, it would be if used continuously. But if used judiciously in combination with other devices and with students who need help with a number of aspects of the reading process, it can be a valuable tool.

---

[8]Dick Cunningham and Scott L. Shablack, "Selective Reading Guide-O-Rama: The Content Teacher's Best Friend," *Journal of Reading, 18* (February, 1975), pp. 380–382.

Figure 4. Signal Words for Pattern Identification[9]

Cause & Effect	Comparison/Contrast	Simple Listing	Time Order
because	however	to begin with . . .	when
since	but	first . . . second . . .	not long after
consequently	yet	next . . .	now
as a result	as well as	then . . .	as
therefore	on the other hand	finally . . .	before
this led to	not only . . . but also		after
so that	while		during
nevertheless	similarly		on (date)
accordingly	either . . . or		by
if . . . then	neither . . . nor		since
			within

Figure 5. Pattern Guide Excerpt* for *The Free and the Brave*, pp. 8–9,[10] Indian Ways of Life—Pattern Guide: Comparison/Contrast

Directions: Read pages 8–9 to be able to complete this chart comparing and contrasting the culture of the Oasis Indians, the Eastern Indians, and you. (A few have been done for you to show you what to do. Complete the rest.)

	YOU	OASIS INDIANS	EASTERN INDIANS
Location	southeastern U.S.		
Types of Work		farmers, house builders, hunters	
Clothing: a) Material			
b) Types			
Men			
Women			
Hair Styles a) Women			
b) Men			
Types of Houses			

*The full guide contains several additional items such as climate, food, transportation, and government.

[9]Richard Vacca, "A means of building comprehension of social studies content," in *Research in Reading in the Content Areas, Second-year Report*, eds., Harold L. Herber and Richard F. Barron (Syracuse, New York: Syracuse University Reading and Language Arts Center, 1973), pp. 75–83.

[10]Graff, *op. cit.*

Figure 6. Guide-O-Rama for *Rise of the American Nation,* Chapter 18[11]

I. A. Read p. 311 *VERY CAREFULLY.* This is a very nice overview
   of the whole chapter. There are 5 sections on this page that will
   be useful to you.

   1. Notice the two key concepts for the chapter in the chapter title
   (blue). Write them below and write a definition of each in your
   own words.

      c_____:

      c_____:

   2. The time period to be discussed in this chapter is given (red). It
   is ____ to ____. (Note: You will notice that the first section
   of the chapter is all about events before 1845. After you read that
   section, see if you can tell why it is important to that time period.)

   3. Read all five paragraphs carefully. This section will give you flavor
   of the period you're going to read about. Do you find any
   indications of sectionalism in this? _____
   What? _____
   _____

   4. "The Chapter Outline" is just that. Note each topic to be covered.
   Can you tell where the chapter is leading? _____
   _____ From this outline, it appears that the materials may tell
   you events leading to a ____ between the North and _____.

   5. Look at the time line. This shows you graphically the time period
   to be considered. The time period would be
   _____-_____.

II. A. Now move on to Section I of this chapter. *Quickly* read the
   following questions *FIRST;* then read the section looking for these
   points:

   1. a) What did the crisis of 1819–1820 involve? (Hint: first
   paragraph) _____
   _____

      b) Whom was the clash between? _____
   and _____

   2. What were the three main provisions of the Missouri Compromise?
   a) _____
   b) _____
   c) _____

   3. What do you think the writers of the textbook meant by "political
   balance" in the title of this section? (Hint: There is not a specific
   definition given in the section. *You* must decide after reading.)

   B. Read "The Tariff Issue" quickly. *Look Out!* You're going to have
   to backtrack to p. 242 for important information—
   READ WITH CARE.

---

[11]Todd and Curti, *op. cit.*

C. *Carefully* look at the map on p. 313.
   1. The title of the map is _____
      _____

   2. Look at the labels on each of the states and the 36° 30′ N. line.
      Are any states above the 36° 30′ N. Compromise line slave
      states? _____ If there are any, list them:
   3. Describe in words what you can tell about the Missouri
      Compromise from this map. _____
      _____
      _____

D. What was the Democratic Party slogan in 1844?
   _____

   How did this slogan help the party politically in the election?
   (Hint: Focus on issues was changed. You tell from what to what!)

III. A. You have just completed the first section of Chapter 18. In
       I.1. you identified and defined the key concepts of the chapter.
       You may wish to go back and change your definitions now.

   Below give all of the examples of crises and compromises you read
   about in this pre-Civil War period.

CRISIS	COMPROMISE

IV. HA HA!! You thought I forgot. I didn't. Go back to "NOTE" in
    in I.2. above and answer the question about the importance of all
    of this to the period of history from 1845–1861.

3. Post-Reading Phase:
Concept/Vocabulary Development

In Figure 1 we listed three major types of activities that might be used to reinforce and extend students' comprehension. Two of those categories, reflective discussion and application activities, include a wide range of possible techniques and experiences which we will not deal with here. Instead, we will focus on the remaining category, vocabulary development exercises.

Word meaning appears to develop through a series of levels or stages. At one level is simple word recognition. This usually involves visual recognition and oral pronunciation. Having a single definition or association for the concept or term is a second level of understanding. When one has a richer set of associations or definitions or can use or make sense of the word in different contexts, then a third level of meaning has been achieved. A major problem in social studies teaching is that too often students do not get beyond the first or perhaps second stage. Take, for example, the term "Jeffersonian democracy." For a historian or social studies teacher it is rich in meaning; for unenlightened students it may have little if any meaning, even though they know in general who Jefferson was and what democracy means. Providing activities and experiences to enrich the meanings students associate with major concepts is an important task of social studies teachers. One way is through vocabulary exercises.

Word Recognition

Word Hunts and Cryptograms. These are easy to create and enjoy wide popularity. To create a cryptogram simply scramble the letters of a series of words having some common association and ask students to spell out the correct words. For the word hunt or hidden word exercise, write the series of words vertically, horizontally, diagonally, etc, and then "hide" the words by surrounding them with other letters. Although, as illustrated in Figure 7, on p. 19, they are most useful as recognition exercises, they may also be constructed as meaning exercises by including a correlated set of descriptions, associations, or definitions.

Meaning Exercises. Word Puzzles: crossword puzzles, central word puzzles (Figure 8, p. 19), and scrambled word exercises (Figure 9, p. 20) can be adapted to a wide range of student abilities. References may be provided to text passages or pages, key letters may be inserted, and so forth to make the puzzles easier to complete. Contrastingly, multiple definitions or less frequently used definitions or associations may be used to help stretch students' understanding of the terms.

Other Activities. Matching-type exercises similar to the matching items on tests, categorization tasks similar to those in concepts guides, and word part or word study exercises focusing on word roots, prefixes, and suffixes are among other useful activities to be considered.

In summary, students' reading comprehension of social studies textbooks continues to be a problem for many teachers. Social studies teachers can continue to throw up their hands in despair, or they can attempt to meet the problem head-on. We have tried to suggest a strategy for organizing textbook-centered instruction and to identify and illustrate some specific activities that may be included in such a strategy.

Figure 7. Word Recognition Exercises

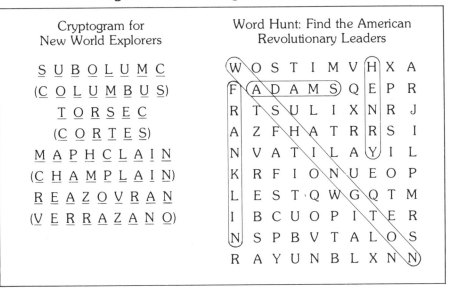

Cryptogram for
New World Explorers

S U B O L U M C
(C O L U M B U S)
T O R S E C
(C O R T E S)
M A P H C L A I N
(C H A M P L A I N)
R E A Z O V R A N
(V E R R A Z A N O)

Word Hunt: Find the American
Revolutionary Leaders

W O S T I M V H X A
F A D A M S Q E P R
R T S U L I X N R J
A Z F H A T R R S I
N V A T I L A Y I L
K R F I O N U E O P
L E S T Q W G Q T M
I B C U O P I T E R
N S P B V T A L O S
R A Y U N B L X N N

Figure 8. Central Word Puzzle

1.   (L I M I T)**E**(D) (R E S O U R C E S)
2.   **C**(A P I T A L I S M)
3.   (G)**O**(O D S)
4.   (D I S T R I B U T I O)**N**
5.   (P R)**O**(D U C T I O N)
6.   (U N L I)**M**(I T E D) (W A N T S)
7.   (S O C)**I** (A L I S M)
8.   (P R I)**C**(E S)
9.   **S** (E R V I C E S)

1. & 6. The basic economic problem confronting all of us and every economic system (#1 is what we have few of and #6 is what we have lots of).

2. The economic system where private ownership predominates.

3. Things that are offered for sale in a market.

4. The term applied to the decision of to whom and how to allocate things in an economic system.

5. An action that results in making available things for the marketplace.

7. The economic system where government ownership of major productive sources prevails.

8. What sellers charge and buyers pay in a market.

9. The other major category available for buying and selling in a market.

Figure 9. Scrambled Word Exercise

I. Rearrange each set of scrambled letters to spell out the name of a person or place important to the exploration of the New World. Use the definitions below to assist you.

1. N E D O L E   D (E) L E O N
2. L O R D D O W L   O L D (W) O R L D
3. T E C I V O S A N   E S T E V A (N) I C O
4. R E T S O C   C O (R) T E S
5. M E D A L S E L L U W E R - (W) A L D S E E M U L L E R
6. C A D E V A   (D) E V A C A
7. O L A B A B   B A (L) B O A
8. B O M C U L S U   C (O) L U M B U S

II. Write the circled letters in order in the spaces provided.

E W N R W D L O

III. Rearrange the letters in II to spell the words which mean the Western Hemisphere (particularly North and South America)

N E W   W O R L D

Definitions

1. First European after the Vikings to land in what is now the United States. Explored Florida in 1513.
2. Eastern Hemisphere (specifically Europe at one time).
3. Most famous black explorer of the New World. Explored with Coronado.
4. Famous conquistador who conquered the Aztecs of Mexico.
5. German geographer whose 1507 book suggested we call the new land "America" after Amerigo Vespucci.
6. First Spaniard to cross the continent of North America.
7. Spanish explorer. Crossed the Isthmus of Panama. First to see the Pacific Ocean.
8. Italian who took the Niña, Pinta, and Santa Maria to the New World in 1492.

Chapter 3

Making the Social Studies Textbook a More Effective Tool for Less Able Readers

Thomas N. Turner

The textbook is probably the most commonly used tool of the elementary teacher for teaching social studies.[1] Thousands of hours of professional time are spent each year in the selection of new social studies textbooks. The professional literature and social studies curriculum classes are often devoted to review and evaluation of social studies textual materials. Most teachers use their textbook in one or in a combination of the following ways (each given, it is hoped, a memorable label):

1. As a *"Bible."* Beginning with chapter one the teacher moves through the textbook, having children read its "gospel" truth and do all (or some) of the suggested activities.
2. As *"Home Land."* The teacher utilizes some additional instructional materials but selects chapters from one text, either independently or in cooperation with children.
3. As *"Tool in a Toolchest"* Multiple texts are used and viewed more as "tools" than as "the program." Inquiring, critical comparison, and adaptation to individual ability and interest are more feasible.

4. As *"76th Trombone."* All available textbooks are used as resources along with a multitude of other resources. The curriculum sequence is provided by the school system, teacher, or pupil-teacher selected topics, problems, or themes.
5. As *"Hood Ornament."* There may be little or no time devoted to social studies, but the textbook is there for the public and supervisors to see.

Textbook writers, state departments of education, and textbook selection committees do not appear to be greatly concerned with the wide variety of instructional functions that textual materials may serve.[2] Even so, the kinds of textbooks needed for each function may vary a great

---

THOMAS N. TURNER is Professor, Department of Curriculum and Instruction, University of Tennessee.

[1]This observation is widely documented. Among more recent substantiating evidence is: James P. Shaver, O.L. Davis, Jr., and Suzanne W. Helburn, "An Interpretive Report on the Status of Pre-College Social Studies" (Washington, D.C.: National Council for the Social Studies, 1978, mimeographed).

[2]Numerous ideas for using texts in a variety of ways are described in Fay Metcalf (Editor), "Using Textbooks Creatively: A Special Section," *Social Education, 44* (Feb. 1980), pp. 84–114.

deal. That variance is part of teaching style. A teacher may be using the textbook as a tool at any of the five functional levels listed above and still be acting in a professional manner and doing a good job of teaching social studies. Since textbook selection is increasingly viewed as a teacher responsibility rather than an administrational one, there is some hope that more importance will be attached to how teachers are going to "fit" textual materials into a program of social studies instruction.

Reading Ability and Textbook Functions

One of the factors that influences the function that a text may serve in a classroom is the ability of children to read that text. Social studies textual materials are most often prepared for the child of average reading ability. For a variety of reasons, many children cannot develop (and others with ability have failed to develop) the reading skills necessary to make effective use of their social studies textbooks. Instructional difficulties in social studies increase as the child gets older. This is because the range of reading abilities becomes greater, and because more textbook reading and more reading independence are expected at each succeeding grade level. The more independent textbook reading that is required and the older the child, the more acute and conspicuous the reading problems become.

Textbook publishers and authors have been acutely aware of readability problems.[3] The amount of supplementary materials and text illustrations, maps, and diagrams has increased and their instructional quality has improved. Specially designed textbooks and easier editions have been published for the less able reader.

But no effort by publishers and authors could ever eliminate the problem entirely. If the reading levels of texts became easy enough for all, they would be too easy for many. Equally important, effective communication of higher-level concepts and gen-

___
[3]Donald O. Schneider and Ronald L. Van Sickle, "The Status of the Social Studies: The Publishers' Perspective," Social Education, 43 (Oct., 1979), p. 464.

eralizations depends on specific, often difficult, vocabulary. Then, too, schools cannot (or will not) always buy all the materials to support texts. The teacher's problem, then, is that many children cannot read with comprehension any textbooks which could be selected to deal with the social studies curriculum. The children's reading problem sets off a chain reaction of frustration, dislike for social studies, and negative learning. Children find that they can only meet school expectations by being "dishonest"—by cheating, copying, getting help. These children lose faith in their own ability to learn in social studies.

Teachers are as much the victim of the textbook reading dilemma as their students. It causes them frustration and boredom, too. Unfortunately, the reading factor, rather than teaching style or instructional goals, limits the functional flexibility of the teacher. Typically, the teacher will try to labor through one textbook as a "Bible" providing maximum instructional help. This use of a text is often repetitive and boring, since many passages are read orally and assignments are gone over tediously. The other alternative that teachers take is the "Hood Ornament" approach, abandoning any thought of the text as a potentially useful instructional instrument. Selective use within one text, multiple texts, and texts as resources is seldom ever tried. It simply demands, the teacher feels, too much expertise.

Reading problems really should not be the factor that controls the function and use of a social studies textbook. The goals of the social studies instructional program and what the teacher deems to be the best instructional approach should be the determinants. This is possible, though, only if the teacher can understand and surmount the reading difficulties.

Analyzing and Understanding Reading Problems

First, the social studies teacher has to know the nature of the reading problems that children encounter with textbooks. These problems are complex and interrelated. But some of these can be identified and dealt with separately. Among the reading difficulties pupils encounter in using social studies textbooks are the following:

A. Children do not have the necessary reading and writing vocabulary. (They may have far better speaking and listening vocabularies.) This means that the teacher is going to have to introduce and explain new concept words, put into visual, concrete form the more abstract terms, have the students keep word files, and provide plenty of vocabulary-building practice and reminders.
B. Children cannot understand questions. This may imply a need to give examples or to develop new and simpler questions or to reduce the number of questions children must answer.
C. Students lack paraphrasing ability. To assure comprehension the teacher is going to have to check repeatedly on the child's ability to put ideas into her/his own words.
D. Children do not have the skills of reading tables, map and chart keys, map scales and symbols. The teacher may have to compensate by doing a great deal of simplification and interpretation.
E. Students have insufficient skills in using glossaries, indexes, tables of contents, appendixes, etc. Special help, practice, and instruction in using these materials will save time and energy for the teacher and the student.
F. Students read slowly or always at the same rate. Skimming and scanning abilities cannot be assumed. The "tricks" of looking for answers and organizational patterns quickly need to be taught.
G. Children have trouble concentrating on reading and are easily distracted. If possible, the social studies teacher needs to cut the length of reading assignments, reduce distraction to a minimum during reading, and assure that reading is done when the student is as fresh and alert as possible.

Other reading and reading study skills are as important, but all of those listed above contribute to reading success and are really within the realm of social studies instruction as well. Careful assessment, instruction, and practice in one or more of the skills separately may improve a child's ability to use better the text as a tool to acquire social studies learnings.

Another preventative measure that teachers can take to better use the social studies text is to assess in advance the reading difficulty of the material. The reading difficulty or readability of social studies texts varies. Publishers will often provide either in the teacher's manual or in literature about the text an average reading grade level for each book in the series. This figure can then be compared to the reading achievement scores of the children. If the information is not given, a school or teacher can also make an estimate of readability by using one of the less complicated readability formulae (the Fry Formula[4] is one that is easily applied). Such formulae have been heavily criticized recently as inadequate measures.[5] However, they still can provide a basis for a rough matching of children with textual materials.

Informal reading inventories[6] may be useful for the social studies teacher who wants to assess individual ability to cope with the *particular* vocabulary, writing style, reading tasks, and other reading aspects of a textbook or chapter. Reading inventories take a variety of forms. One basic procedure may consist of an individual session with a child in which he or she orally reads a selection from the reading material to the teacher. The teacher keeps a record of the number and the kind of oral reading errors made by the child. Then a series of questions is asked by the teacher to gain an estimate of the child's understanding of what has been read. Typically, the series of teacher questions probes at: (1) recall of detail, (2) general understanding, (3) vocabulary meaning, (4) recall of sequence, and (5) ability to make inferences from reading. The entire process may take only a few minutes and the competent teacher can gain a rough estimate of the child's ability to cope with the reading difficulty of the text. The same procedure can be adapt-

[4]Edward Fry, "A Readability Formula That Saves Time," *Journal of Reading*, 11 (April, 1968), pp. 513–517, 574–577.
[5]Alvin Gronowski and Morton Botel, "Background for a New Syntactic Complexity Formula," *The Reading Teacher*, 28 (October, 1974), pp. 31–35.
[6]For an outstanding analysis of this approach, see John Pikulski, "A Critical Review: Informal Reading Inventories, *The Reading Teacher*, 28 (November, 1974), pp. 141–151.

ed to assess flexibility of reading rate, map and graph skills, and many of the other reading skills necessary for success in using a textbook.

Working With and Around Reading Problems

Assessment of the reading difficulty of the social studies text may, of course, lead to the conclusion that it is too difficult for independent reading by many of the children in the class. There may not be sufficient social studies class time to devote to assessment and development of specific requisite reading skills. Should the teacher be able and willing to work with the children on needed reading skills, this may take a considerable period of time. Reading difficulties still need not limit the use of social studies textbooks as important social learning tools appropriate to a flexible range of functions. There is a variety of activities, tactics, and techniques which can enable the social studies teacher, at least to some degree, to work around the reading difficulties. Selection, development, and use of particular ideas appropriate for a given class depend upon a number of factors including individual teaching style, classroom organization pattern, resources available, the learning style and independent work abilities of students, and, probably most important, the flexibility and creativity of the teacher.

A number of briefly developed technique ideas follow. No pretense is made at describing these techniques thoroughly. Many examples and much descriptive detail could be written about each. The purpose here is only to demonstrate the range of possibilities. It is hoped that each technique is presented sufficiently for it to serve as a "jogger" or starter-idea for a competent and creative social studies teacher.

A. Tape record, on cassettes, readings of critically important textbook sections. If earphones or headsets are available, allow groups of children who have difficulty with the text to "read it" by listening. If multiple headsets are not available, it may be possible to find a place where the sound will not disturb. (Able readers might even be able to help in making the recordings.)

Children can follow along in their texts as they listen. References to text pictures, maps, etc. can be given more emphasis. The reading selections can also be broken into briefer sections with more frequent questioning than the text uses itself. The teacher is then free to work with other children, yet may be nearby and accessible for any need.

B. Have two children do textbook reading assignments together, assisting one another with reading problems. If one child is a superior reader, have him or her read short sections to the less able reader and then let the latter review what was read. This should be less damaging to the self-concept of the poor readers than failing at reading. They are serving in a helper relationship and doing something at which they can succeed. The teacher does need to take sensible safeguards toward matching children who will help one another, rather than engage in battles for ego security and superiority.

C. Prepare or have children who are capable of reading the text prepare summaries and outlines of textbook sections. These may serve as review aids for all children. In actual practice, they will *be* the "textbook" for the children incapable of reading the text. Outstanding summaries can be used year after year. Poor readers may even be able to take part in the writing of these, if these children have been involved in one of the two activities described above by using a language-experience writing technique or by recording their summaries. If not, they may make valuable contributions to the "library" of summaries and outlines in other ways—illustrating; binding; writing captions, questions, and headings; etc.

D. Develop question-asking skills by having less able readers ask questions about textbook illustrations. (First attempts will be obvious-answer or low-significance questions involving literal observation of what the children actually see.) Picture analysis is, of course, a difficult and demanding skill. With less able readers, though, questions about pictures may be used to focus attention on what the textual portion of the social study book is about.

Recent research attaches great importance to the ability to predict and anticipate as a means to reading comprehension.[7] Children can also be led to better questioning by using a variation of Manzo's "ReQuest" questioning technique[8] with pictures. In this approach the teacher acts as a model, alternately asking a question which the child answers and then hearing a child ask a question which the teacher answers.

E. Have the class as a whole prepare a "cartoon" narrative of part of the text, depicting the major concepts developed in cartoon form. Each frame might represent a single idea, a paragraph, or a section. Cartoons can also be used singly to illustrate abstract concepts. Either the children can draw their own cartoons or they can collect favorite comic strips or cartoons, cover the conversation "balloons" with white paper, and then write in their own narrative portion. This may help make abstract ideas more concrete and present narrative aspects of the social studies. If neither drawn nor collected cartoons suffice, something like the "Invisible Tribe" idea from "Dick Tracy," where there are no real pictures, only imaginary ones, may be a device for developing the relationships of visual imagination to verbal passage. Cartoons used this way can also be an avenue to discussing the political and social commentary of cartoons in the media.

F. Cut pictures from old textbooks as well as other resources and have low reading-ability children relate these to illustrations, maps, headings, and other aspects of the texts they are using. Unit scrapbooks and bulletin boards are among the outlets for using these pictures. Less able readers can be involved in matching the sequence of the scrapbook or bulletin board to that of the text. In a sense this kind of activity represents a way of "visual paraphrasing" and should enhance comprehension, serve as review material, and provide alternative associations to aid memory.

G. Treat sections of the text in a "language experience" fashion, developing from the children a sequence of sentences in their own words. The teacher writes these sentences verbatim. Children's descriptions can be used for reading lessons relative to the conceptual or factual content of the text. This is an obvious advantage in that the textual descriptions are in those language patterns familiar to the child. In addition, the child has had a valuable listening experience before facing the reading material.

H. Develop "textbook learning centers" where groups of children are each responsible for developing learning experiences for the other children for a small section of a chapter. All of the "centers" together will provide the total chapter. After the centers have been developed each child can be "processed" through all the centers.

The nature of the "centers" will depend upon the textual content and focus. One approach is to assign each group one or more subheadings from the text. The groups might then be asked to develop different sets of learning activities. For example, one group might make a collection of pictures with questions about each; another might make event-sequence, vegetation, rainfall, elevation, and/or product map dittos with region-dividing or comparative activities for the students who go through the center; another group might design a simulated archaeological "dig" or replica of the culture with activities which would enable the learners to do inquiry thinking, draw conclusions, and make decisions about the economy, culture, history, and life of the group of people described in the text; and yet another might make timelines with activities and questions to accompany them. A different way to structure the group-made centers is to have them task-oriented. Each group pulls from the entire chapter a particular aspect. One group could be charged with visualizing vocabulary, another with developing map learning, another with time concepts. Regardless of how the centers are structured, it is probably best to structure and specify the tasks in as much detail as possible until (or unless) the independence of the groups can be developed.

---

[7]J. Estil Alexander, et al., *Teaching Reading* (Boston: Little, Brown and Co., 1979), pp. 135–136.

[8]Anthony V. Manzo, "The ReQuest Procedure," *Journal of Reading, 13* (November, 1969), pp. 123–126.

I. Try "key word" and "key name" hunts where children search indexes and chapters for words of high conceptual value or significant proper nouns and then only have to read enough to describe these key words. This minimizes the necessary reading and develops both skimming and scanning skills along with vocabulary. From the "hunts" children can make word banks or files with which they can be encouraged to develop a "collector's" motivation of accumulation.

Conclusion

Teachers who wish to work effectively using a social studies text that is beyond the reading abilities of classes or individuals must be willing to go beyond the text. They must find approaches which simplify and structure textbook use. Beginning with careful assessment of the reading difficulty of textual materials, matching assigned pupil tasks to the student's ability to do the necessary reading is of absolute necessity. The length of reading assignments should be kept within the attention span of the students, and frustration resulting from too long or too difficult reading should be avoided. The distraction levels of the children and the distraction factors present when the children are reading social studies texts should be given consideration.

The reading experience itself should be guided. Enough help and instruction should be given to meet the demands of the children's ability to work alone and independently. Copywork assignments and work which demands parrot-like response about uncomprehended passages are counter-productive to learning and motivation. Frustration, boredom, and cheating are more likely results of such work.

The less able reader depends more on teachers. He/she needs assistance, discussion, and help with specialized or new vocabulary previous to reading. Provision of visual and other sensory experiences which teach the abstract and/or verbally described concepts of the text is also required by poor readers. Work and guidance with skimming and scanning, group review and synthesis discussion, practice in and exposure to paraphrasing and summarizing of the social studies texts are all essential aids for the child with reading difficulty.

For the reader who is unable to read independently a social studies text, it is as important as it is for the capable reader, and perhaps even more important, that a purpose be provided for using and reading the text. That purpose must be made personally meaningful and significant so that the child will want to at least *try* to read.

Though reading ability is important for utilizing social studies texts effectively, insufficient reading skills should not limit normal social studies instruction. By careful planning and reduction of activities which do not contribute to learning, texts can be utilized in almost limitless ways. Sometimes actual reading may be reduced. Even so, social studies texts can and should be useful tools for the development of the social concepts of even the less able reader.

Chapter 4

How To Read Pictures

Martin W. Sandler

Somebody once said that one picture is worth a thousand words. We don't intend to take issue with that adage, but we would like to extend the discussion by saying that some pictures can speak a thousand words or more, provided that the viewer can understand the language of pictures.

Just as a beautifully written Russian or Indian song would have little meaning for a non-linguist, so, too, the person who fails to grasp the artist/photographer's intent misses the meaning of the picture. And although a thousand words may have been poured into that picture by the artist, only a few of them will be understood by the viewer if he or she can't read pictures.

We feel that there is definitely a picture language, and that it is an important language to know, not just because it will help you and your students to appreciate their textbooks, but also because it will provide better insight into our highly visual world. Fortunately, it is not a difficult language to learn. Almost everyone can master it, especially the more visually sensitive learners.

Pictures in General

As you know, most textbooks are full of large, descriptive pictures. Most of them are loaded with information. Many of them show a point of view on some issue, or idea, or person. Some of the pictures are realistic, others idealistic, a few futuristic. Hardly any of the pictures are alike, but they all

have two things in common. One, they are photographs. Two, they were all chosen by the author or art editors from thousands of pictures.

The different kinds of photographs one might find in a textbook would include:

1. a photo of a painting
2. a photo of a cartoon
3. a photo of a statue or building
4. a photo of an advertisement
5. a photo of a drawing
6. a posed photograph
7. an action photo
8. a photo of a model
9. a photo of a movie
10. a photo of someone's creation

It is worthwhile to know that there are different kinds of photographs in a textbook, and that the pictures were taken for a variety of reasons and can be read separately or individually.

Asking Questions of Pictures

1. *What kind of picture is it?* Is it an illustration, a photo, a chart, a map, or a combination of these, like an illustrative map?

    If it is a photo . . .

2. *What kind of photo is it?* Refer to the list above.

    If the picture is a photograph of a painting, for example, then . . .

3. *Why didn't the photographer shoot the picture himself or herself?* Is it because the scene predates the photographer, like the Battle on Lexington Green or Christopher Columbus's arrival in the New World? Or is it that the artist captured something on canvas which the photographer wants to picture, like a

MARTIN W. SANDER has taught for more than twenty years at every level from junior high to college, and he has served as coordinator of social studies for Newton and Wayland, Massachusetts, public school systems.

Saturday Evening Post cover by Norman Rockwell?

If the photographer shoots the picture himself . . .

4. *Is he or she objectively reporting what was seen, or is he or she making a personal comment?* Has the photographer photographed the complete scene, or merely one side of it? In other words, would you see both sides of the battlefield, or only the victorious American army?

If the photographer is making a personal comment . . .

5. *What exactly is the photographer saying in the picture?* Does he or she catch a political figure in an absurd pose or show one of our large cities smothered in smog or picture a young American soldier being decorated for bravery in Vietnam? There are so many ways a photographer can put across his or her point of view. It is essential for the viewer to see the angle clearly.

6. *What has the photographer left out of the picture?* Is the viewer seeing enough of the scene, or have certain details been cropped out of the picture? A photograph is only a part of the total scene, and the viewer must keep in mind that there may be details left out of the picture which could alter its meaning.

For example, below is a portion of a full picture that appears in a text, and then the full picture is presented on the next page.

How is your interpretation of the picture changed by seeing the full picture?

7. *What is actually in the picture?* When a
person first looks at a photo, he or she
may not see what's there. Too often we
give pictures a glance instead of sub-
jecting them to close scrutiny. This is
especially true of pictures in textbooks.
The photos in a textbook must be
looked at carefully if all that is in them
is to be absorbed by the viewer. But how
do we know if we are seeing everything
that is in the picture? Let's go through
the mental process of examining a
photo and see. [Study the photograph
on pages 30–31.]

Library of Congress

Mental Process of Reading Pictures

After studying the photo for awhile, you can begin to focus on what is in the picture. You and some of your students can move rather rapidly through the process; but for the majority of the students, we suggest a moderate pace. Eventually the process can become second nature to a student.

Developing mastery in the mental process of reading pictures is similar to other mental processes, as you will see from the following:

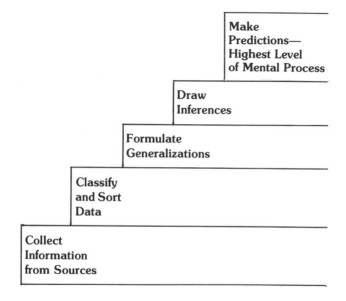

Let's focus on the photo of the painting of the Battle of Tippecanoe, and go through the process to see what's *in* the picture. Not every picture can take the viewer to the level of making predictions, but go with it as far as the picture will take you. Obviously some pictures are deeper in content than others.

Collecting Data

This activity can be as sophisticated as the skill level of the students. To get a full view of the spectrum, we will approach it simply by starting off with the basic skill of listing. Using the picture of the Battle of Tippecanoe [pp. 30–31], make a list of:

The number of people in the picture . . . . . approx. 50

The number of animals . . . . one horse

Things that grow . . . trees
grass
ferns

Type of action . . . . battle scene

Types of clothing . . . uniforms
buckskin

Tools and/or weapons rifles
swords
hatchets
spears
bows, arrows

Classifying and Sorting Data

A *classification matrix* is an ideal method for classifying and sorting information. It is not necessary to construct one for every picture, but it is a helpful tool and can be utilized over and over again. At first the teacher should provide the headings. Classifying is a good way of telling whether or not students are learning.

Kinds of Action	Kinds of Clothing	Kinds of People
shooting	hats	Indians
aiming	coats	foot soldiers
falling	belts	an officer
talking	capes	American army
leading	blankets	all men
crawling	shirts	young
tossing	feathers	
hiding	pants	
helping	moccasins	
killing	necklaces	
dying	pouches	
fleeing		
carrying		
riding		

Formulating Generalizations

A generalization is a statement of fact based upon information gathered, classified, and sorted. Students should be encouraged to generalize from data. Of course, at times the data may be inaccurate, but the mental process of formulating generalizations is still valid. Some generalizations about the picture of the Battle of Tippecanoe:

- The Indians and American soldiers are about equal in numbers.
- The American soldiers have superior firepower.
- The Indians are making a brave charge.
- Both sides are suffering heavy casualties.
- The Indian forces are losing the battle.

Drawing Inferences

An inference is a probability statement derived from facts, information, observations, and insight. It is a higher level of productive thinking than formulating generalizations, because, as you will see, it draws conclusions from all the data.

Drawing inferences about the picture of the Battle of Tippecanoe:

- The American soldiers will win the battle.
- When you have superior firepower, there is no need to be afraid that you will lose.

Making Predictions

So far, students have been taught and encouraged to draw conclusions from sifted evidence, and that is an accomplishment. But in order for a person to climb to the level of prediction, he or she must go beyond the evidence and draw conclusions from unknowns. In other words, he or she must demonstrate the power to estimate, to guess within reasonable boundaries, and to judge.

Some predictions based on the Tippecanoe picture:

- American soldiers will probably defeat the Indians in battle.
- Indians will do everything they can to replace hatchets, arrows, and spears with rifles.
- American settlers in this area will need military protection.

Going through the activities and exercises in the *Mental Process of Reading Pictures* will help the viewer see more clearly what is actually in a picture. Of course, not every picture in a textbook can be as richly mined as the Tippecanoe photo, but nonetheless students should be encouraged to ask questions of pictures. Most of them have a lot to say.

Again, we want to stress the point that students who have difficulty reading the written word can read pictures, and may be able to read them better than other students.

The Author's Bias

Almost everybody has a point of view, even objective authors. They take a stand in their textbooks on many issues, and this stand may be even more evident visually than verbally. Authors and editors have thousands of pictures to choose from. Remember, one of the questions to ask of a photo is: What has the photographer left out of his or her picture? A similar question might be asked of the author: What pictures were left out of the book? For if students are going to become skillful at reading pictures, they should know that the pictures that they are viewing are probably not the only ones of the scenes depicted.

Although we may never learn which pictures were discarded, we might, if we study the text thoroughly, discern why many of the pictures were included. Making such predictions could be a worthy challenge for some students.

Chapter 5

Correcting Sex Stereotypes in Textbooks

William E. Patton

DIMENSIONS OF
SEX-ROLE STEREOTYPING

For more than a decade, the problem of sex-role stereotyping in social studies textbooks has received public attention. Special interest groups have brought the problem into the political arena as well as the educational arena. The weight of law, however, has not been fully felt in correcting sex-role stereotypes. Some people had hoped that the Title IX rules and regulations, which were published in the *Federal Register* on Wednesday, June 4, 1975, and were approved to eliminate any discrimination on the basis of sex in educational programs, would include textbooks and curricular materials. This hope was not realized. The document spoke for itself: "Nothing in this regulation shall be interpreted as requiring or prohibiting or abridging in any way the use of particular textbooks or curricular materials."[1] Prog-

ress, therefore, toward the removal of stereotypes based on sex in social studies textbooks has been slow.

Many textbooks published from 1977 through 1980 for use in social studies classrooms have made noticeable changes to correct sexist elements. The scope of the problem requires more than additional illustrations and the use of nonsexist language, however. It may be helpful to examine the spectrum of direct and indirect dimensions of sex-role stereotyping in social studies textbooks. The following list of questions is not exhaustive; yet, it does communicate the complexity of the problem.

Do textbooks and curricular materials:

1. illustrate or describe females engaged in passive settings, while illustrating or describing males engaged in vigorous activities?

[1]*Federal Register*, June 4, 1975.

2. use masculine subsuming language to describe a hypothetical person?
3. show or describe females as followers or under the direction of males disproportionately to males as followers or under the direction of females?
4. characterize female interests as self, home, and school, while characterizing male interests as community and world?
5. give disproportionate coverage to the roles and problems of males compared to the roles and problems of females?
6. describe the female emotional character as flighty and insecure, while describing the male emotional character as stable and secure?
7. have males as main characters or exemplary persons disproportionately in relation to having females as main characters or exemplary persons?
8. show males more frequently in illustrations, individually and in groups, than show females in similar settings?
9. illustrate or describe females in occupations that are principally nurturing in nature, while illustrating or describing males in high status and/or instrumental career roles?
10. show males in affiliate relationships that result in action, while females are shown as unaffiliated?
11. define female identity by using a male as the reference?

This list of questions can be beneficial as a starting point to identify criteria for analyzing social studies textbooks for sexist elements.

ANALYSIS FOR SEXIST ELEMENTS

A belief that sex stereotypes are present in social studies textbooks does not provide the documentation needed to establish the problem as fact. A weakness of some analysis techniques is their reliance on simple checklists and qualitative judgments. The need exists in most classrooms for reliable information concerning the differential treatment of females and males. For teachers and students to make informed decisions about the presence of sex-role stereotypes, they need a solid information base. The procedure that follows relies on a quantitative analysis using ratios to document the differential treatment of males and females.

The specific criteria for analyzing social studies textbooks for sexist elements are selected from the questions listed above. To generate the data that will make it possible for teachers and students to use sexist textbooks in non-stereotypic ways, it is not necessary to ask all eleven questions. For the purposes of this chapter, four criteria will be used: (1) language, (2) occupations, (3) illustrations, and (4) roles.

Language

The language criterion has been selected as the first focus for analysis because of the emphasis it has received from critics. Publishers, feminists, and academics have been concerned about the problem of language in sex-role stereotyping throughout the 1970s. One of the most lucid and helpful publications in the area was written by Robin Lakoff.[2] Her book, *Language and Woman's Place,* highlights two dimensions of the differential treatment received by females through linguistic discrimination. The way women are taught to use language is one dimension, and the other is the manner in which language treats women.

Robin Lakoff describes the use of euphemistic terms to characterize women's work; e.g., household engineer. No one is publicly searching for alternative words to describe roles traditionally dominated by men, such as bank president, professor, or doctor. Yet how many different terms have been developed in recent years for the role of "housewife"? Language is symptomatic of a deeper problem.

> The presence of the words is a signal that something is wrong, rather than (as too often interpreted by well-meaning reformers) the problem itself. The point here is that . . . we [must] start feeling more respect for women and, at the same time, less uncomfortable about them and their roles in society in relation to men. . . .[3]

An obvious point to consider when analyzing social studies textbooks is that the

[2]R. Lakoff, *Language and Woman's Place* (New York: Harper and Row, 1975).
[3]*Ibid.,* p. 21.

term "man" should not describe men *and* women. The general use of nouns and pronouns usually subsumes females to hypothetical males. Much of the writing used in social studies classrooms at all levels is nonfiction. There is a debate in the literature concerning the use of nonsexist language in fiction and nonfiction writings.[4] The intent of this criterion is not planned to restrict the use of language in appropriate fiction; rather, it is planned to use language in a nondiscriminatory manner in nonfiction.

Table 1 is the basic worksheet for analyzing textbooks using the language criterion. The initial step in using the worksheet is the identification of three sample sections from the social studies textbook. By dividing the text into thirds and using a tab marker, the analyst can make a selection of one sample from each third. As many as ten pages may be needed in elementary textbooks (some first-grade items can be read in their entirety), while fewer pages may be needed in secondary geography or government textbooks. Every masculine and feminine noun and pronoun must be recorded for each sample. If the pronoun "she" is used five times, then the pronoun would be written once and four tally marks would follow the word. A sample dealing with nomads might include words such as "woman," "kinsmen," "him" and "her." Another sample from the Middle Ages might produce "lords," "countess," "king," "churchmen," "she," and "queen." (See p. 38.)

When the appropriate words have been recorded, the column totals are summed for all words and then for nouns and pronouns separately. The final step in the analysis using the language criterion is the computation of ratios. This figure is determined most easily by dividing the smallest number into the largest number; i.e., masculine nouns *18* and feminine nouns *6* equals a 3 to 1 ratio, or feminine pronouns *30* and masculine pronouns *15* equals a 2 to 1 ratio. It is important to note the direc-

tion of the ratio regarding its reflection of a masculine or feminine dominance. Ratios that deviate from the ideal ratio of 1 to 1 may indicate differential treatment. The 1 to 1 ratio is an ideal standard and provides a starting point when interpreting the outcome of an analysis.

The historical record described in most elementary and secondary textbooks is the story of male history. This reality speaks as much to the bias of authors and publishers as it does to "real" history. The current state of history available for classrooms in textbooks will produce ratios that are heavily dominated by masculine nouns and pronouns. Present conditions will remain until "androgynous history" is written from a human perspective rather than from the female or male point of view.[5]

Occupations

The stereotypic nature of career-role models presented in textbooks has been a popular focus for general writers in education and for researchers. Because of their efforts, classroom teachers can be aware of the problem and its impact on students. One writer while analyzing textbooks used in grades 1 through 10 prepared a list of female career roles and male career roles found in the books.[6] One hundred and eighteen were listed for females and 492 for males. The ratio of 4.2 to 1 is not uncommon in social studies textbooks.

A more disturbing fact documented by researchers is the impact of sex-role stereotypes of occupations on students. Schlossberg and Goodman found that elementary students, when interviewed regarding the appropriateness of specific jobs for men and women, rejected women from men's jobs more often than they rejected men from jobs traditionally held by women.[7] The writers concluded that children

[4]C. S. Johnson and G. R. Greenbaum, "Aren't Standards Always Used? A Reply to Kingston and Lovelace," *Journal of Reading Behavior* (1979), pp. 73–77.

[5]A. Chapman, "Women in the History Curriculum," *The Social Studies* (May/June 1978), pp. 117–121.

[6]G. Britton, "Sex Stereotypes and Career Roles," *Journal of Reading* (November 1973), pp. 140–148.

[7]N. K. Schlossberg and J. Goodman, "A Woman's Place: Children's Sex Stereotypes of Occupations," *Vocational Guidance Quarterly* (June 1972), pp. 266–270.

Table 1

Criterion One: **Are females subsumed to males because of words used to characterize a hypothetical person?**

	Masculine	Feminine
Sample 1 pp. ———		
Sample 2 pp. ———		
Sample 3 pp. ———		
	Total ——— Nouns ——— Pronouns ———	Total ——— Nouns ——— Pronouns ———

	Real	Ideal
Overall Male to Female Ratio	———	1:1
Noun Ratio	———	1:1
Pronoun Ratio	———	1:1

placed greater limitations on occupations available to women than to men. It should be noted that factors such as the home and media contribute to children's perceptions of appropriate career roles. Textbooks, however, should avoid reinforcing the stereotypes.

Use of the occupation criterion to analyze social studies textbooks requires a two-dimensional analysis. Textbook reviewers have found an additional factor that influences career-role stereotypes. Some occupations are *expressive* while others are *instrumental*. The expressive includes the nurturing and service roles such as teacher, nurse, clerk, and librarian. Production and equipment manipulation occupations such as those of construction worker, laboratory technician, and logger are examples of the instrumental. Although the two categories do not allow for the classification of all occupations, they are convenient for attaining another level of analysis. Women and men may be shown equally in expressive roles. The same will not be true regarding instrumental occupations—men dominate the category.

Unlike the previous criterion, the entire social studies textbook is used to complete Table 2 The content analysis uses the pictures in the book. Very few occupations with a gender reference are included in textbook narratives apart from pictorial representations. Illustrations include photographs, drawings, and other visuals. When the sex of a person is questionable because the figure is partially hidden or poorly illustrated, the example should not be written in the appropriate column for sex. The judgment of the analyst (teacher or student) is critical for each classification. For example, a female doctor using a brain scanner would be classified as female and instrumental. A male doctor seated behind a desk and listening to a patient would be recorded in the male/expressive cell. What the person is doing as part of the occupational role is as important as the occupation itself. (See p. 40.)

Totals and ratios are determined in the same way as those for Criterion One. The ideal ratio of 1 to 1 for language is very much an abstraction, something to be at-

tained in the future. Conversely, the occupation criterion ratio should be attainable now. Laws regulate all exclusionary aspects of occupations in the United States. The interaction of tradition and sexist biases is no longer legal grounds for restricting a woman or man from any occupation. Few of the thousands of occupations available during the 1980s can legitimately exclude anyone on the basis of sex as a single criterion. By correcting career-role stereotypes, the United States can develop into a country of equal employment opportunity.

Illustrations

Demographers report that slightly over 50 percent of our population is made up of females. The photographs, paintings, and cartoons in social studies textbooks reflect a female to male ratio quite different from the true distribution of population by sex. Males are depicted in visual presentations more often than females. With textbooks second only to teachers and peers as a socializing force in schools, the differential representation of females in illustrations continues to reinforce the image of women as the subordinate sex.

Another way to view the preponderance of male illustrations in social studies textbooks is to consider it as a form of propaganda. Authors and publishers might disagree with this contention, but (whether by design or default) textbooks are systematic in their biased presentation of women and men in illustrations. Advertisers have used pictures to propagandize consumers toward specific economic behavior for years. Ignoring the influence of stereotypic illustrations will not reduce the magnitude of the problem.

Gathering information from a textbook to complete Table 3 is somewhat simpler than the previous procedures. First, an illustration will fall into one of two categories based on the number of people shown. Either one person is displayed or a group is presented visually. Group pictures often communicate an important sex-role stereotype. How often are females shown as the majority in a group picture where men and women are both presented? Women as nu-

Table 2

Criterion Two: **Are females shown disproportionately in expressive occupations, while males are shown disproportionately in instrumental occupations?**

	Males	Females
Expressive		
Instrumental		
	Total Number _____ Expressive _____ Instrumental _____	Total Number _____ Expressive _____ Instrumental _____

	Real	Ideal
Overall Male to Female Ratio	_____	1:1
Expressive Ratio	_____	1:1
Instrumental Ratio	_____	1:1

Table 3

Criterion Three: **Are females shown in illustrations disproportionately to males?**

	Males	Females	Group Males	Group Females	Group Balance
Photographs					
Paintings/ Cartoons/ Drawings					
	Total ___ Photos ___ Others ___	Total ___ Photos ___ Others ___	Total ___ Photos ___ Others ___	Total ___ Photos ___ Others ___	

	Real	Ideal		Real	Ideal
Single Male to Female Ratio	___	1:1	Photo Ratio	___	1:1
			Other Ratio	___	1:1
Group Male to Female Ratio	___	1:1	Photo Ratio	___	1:1
			Other Ratio	___	1:1

merical minorities in group illustrations become subordinate. They do not have the opportunity to be shown in relationships where the female is the majority. A secondary social studies book published less than two years ago had a 6 to 1 group male-to-female ratio. (See p. 41.)

A second factor to consider when using Table 3 is the type of illustration. Photographs have been isolated because they tend to be the most common visual form used in social studies textbooks. Some major exceptions have been published at the primary level by using drawings as the only illustrations. One type of illustration might have an ideal ratio while the other reflects a bias. A tally mark is placed in the appropriate cell for each illustration. For some secondary social studies textbooks a 75–100-page sample from three random sections of the book can be used. A division procedure similar to the one described for Criterion One will help.

The ratios for Table 3 are computed for single and group illustrations. They are also figured for the two types of visuals for the single column and group column. A total of six ratios is determined in completing the table.

Roles

The fourth analysis criterion—roles—is more difficult to isolate than the other three. Its imprecision is not a definitional problem, but a result of the broad scope of the criterion when applied to social studies textbooks. One dimension of role might address the psychological attributes of active and passive. Another might be the sex of the main characters presented in a textbook's narrative. The parochial or world view of females and males is a third possibility. The sex of the main characters will be used as the basis for establishing the fourth analysis criterion.

The handling of main characters has been selected because of the focus on people in social studies textbooks. For example, primary-grade students might study Marie and her Puerto Rican family in New York City. The work of Louis Leakey might be described in a middle-school textbook. Finally, Angelina and Sarah Grimké might (or might not) be discussed in a high-

school United States history book. The choices authors make about which hypothetical and/or real people to include in a textbook must, necessarily, exclude some individuals. The fourth criterion will allow the teachers and students examining the texts to identify sexist patterns in the authors' choices.

Textbooks can be entered at a variety of points to gather information for Table 4. In some cases it will be necessary to read the narrative. Elementary social studies textbooks can be analyzed in this manner. Other texts have biographical features that focus on significant personalities. These are usually listed as one part of the table of contents. One textbook detailed the lives of significant scientists throughout history. The analysis identified one woman (Marie Curie) and eighteen men. Some people might argue that the 18 to 1 male-dominated ratio reflects reality. Unfortunately, individuals advocating this position are speaking more from their own ignorance than from a knowledge of contributions to the development of science. Finally, the index can be studied for people's names. The index is most valuable when analyzing history texts used at the elementary and secondary levels. Regardless of which entry point is used, each individual's name is written on the analysis sheet. (See p. 43.)

Some textbooks will be entirely nonfiction. Others may include some fictional characters. Fiction writing is useful in textbooks to communicate social studies facts, concepts, and generalizations. By placing an asterisk next to each fictional person, it is possible to document any differential treatment that might be systematic on the basis of the fictional or nonfictional nature of the female and male characters. Each column is summed and a ratio is computed.

Employing one or more of the analysis sheets to document sex-role stereotypes in social studies textbooks is the first step in using the materials in nonsexist ways. The ratios from all four sheets provide a more complete profile than just one or two. The set of sheets, when used correctly, can provide the information needed by teachers and students to counteract sex-role stereotypes.

Table 4

Criterion Four: **Are females presented as main characters disproportionately to males?**

Males	Females
Total _____	Total _____

Real   Ideal

Overall Male to Female Ratio _____   1:1

CORRECTING
SEXIST TEXTBOOK IMAGES

The transition from knowing a textbook is sexist to correcting it in the classroom involves an important human element. This is the internal consciousness on the part of teachers that the fact of sexist textbooks is a problem. Several years ago a national organization published an excellent article in its journal concerning the stereotypic nature of illustrations. Two months later the journal published a letter to the editor from a high-school biology teacher who commented on the earlier article. A concluding barb from the teacher asked if the writer of the article didn't have something better to do than count pictures. This teacher's attitude reflects both the importance and difficulty of the issue.

The attitude of teachers toward the existence of sexist social studies textbooks is important because the lives of millions of young people are being influenced in subtle and not so subtle ways. Either through their own bigotry, a lack of appropriate staff development activities, or unenlightened contact with current educational literature, some teachers have failed to internalize the problem. Without significant steps to heighten their consciousness, little can be done to correct the stereotypic images.

The steps outlined below have been planned with teachers in mind who know the problem exists and are sufficiently concerned to work toward making a change. For this group, documenting the fact of sexist materials is the first step and motivation for correcting the images. Several excellent pieces of literature are available to help social studies teachers understand the scope of the problem and identify alternatives for correcting it.[8]

_____
[8]P. Gough, *Sexism: New Issue in American Education* (Bloomington, IN: Phi Delta Kappa, 1976); M. Guttentag and H. Bray, *Undoing Sex Stereotypes: Research and Resources for Educators* (New York: McGraw-Hill, 1976); M. E. Reilly, "Eliminating Sexism: A Challenge to Educators," *Social Education* (April 1979), pp. 312–316; *Social Studies* (May/June 1978), pp. 91–129; Stacey, Bereaud, and Daniels, *And Jill Came Tumbling After* (New York: Dell, 1974).

Correction Starts with the Stereotype

The analysis sheets illustrated earlier are useful for teachers and older students. They can use the sheets to engage in a form of action research in the classroom. Questions and hypotheses raised in the course of instruction regarding sex-role stereotypes set the conditions, the analysis sheets provide the technique, and discussion of the results in relation to the conditions serves as the outcome. Teachers and students are able to join together to identify sex-role stereotypes.

A careful description of each stereotype in a textbook is important. This does not mean each instance of a stereotype; a teacher would be making descriptive statements dozens of times with some materials. Rather, the results of an analysis sheet are put into narrative form.

SPRINGBOARD LESSONS

Even though the Springboard Lessons developed for this chapter focus on the problem of sex stereotyping of females in social studies textbooks, the problem is not limited to females. The techniques described in the section on analysis for sexist elements may produce information regarding the stereotypic portrayal of males. Students may find it interesting to examine the analysis results to identify patterns of mutual differential treatment. That is, when males are shown as unrealistically heroic, are females shown as particularly weak? Most stereotypes have negative parallels for both sexes. (**Springboard Lessons appear on pp. 45–47.**)

Springboard Lesson 1 is designed for use in primary-grade social studies. The occupation criterion was used to document the sexist nature of the textbook. In primary grades, teachers need to expose the students to role models showing both sexes in expressive and instrumental roles. Excellent supplementary materials which depict women and men in nonsexist occupational roles are now available for primary classrooms.[9]

SPRINGBOARD LESSON 1

Primary—Occupations

Description:

How many women go on picnics wearing skirts and high-heeled shoes? How many girls swing, ride bikes, and play ball wearing dresses? These are some of the visual images presented to primary children in one textbook. Another characterizes females in occupations with equal bias. Thirteen women are shown in 12 occupations while 34 men are depicted in 21 occupations. All of the women are in expressive career roles except two. No men have expressive jobs; 12 have instrumental jobs. The only positive aspect of the occupations for women is the illustration of a minority female in an instrumental role as a dentist. The students reading these textbooks will see women in stereotyped roles which reflect a narrower range of career opportunities for women than those available for men.

Objective:

The students will identify the diverse occupations women have in the community the school serves.

Activities:

1. Bring a resource person into the classroom. An employment counselor from the State Employment Agency would be desirable. If this type of person is not available in your community, then a high school counselor or an employee of a private employment agency might be used. The resource person could outline and describe the various jobs that women have taken in the community. The students should have preplanned questions ready for the resource person on career options for females and males.
2. The students could describe the jobs held by various female members of their families. Pictures could be cut from magazines to illustrate the occupations. These pictures could be used to construct bulletin boards or design occupation collages.
3. The children might take a field trip to a local industrial plant or other type of facility where women are employed in instrumental roles (identify a site where men are employed in expressive roles). The students should be encouraged to identify the number of occupations that men and women have that are the same; i.e., a woman and man operating a drill press side by side.

Information Source:

Wertheimer, B.M. *We Were There: The Story of Working Women in America.* New York: Pantheon Books, 1977.

---

[9]*People at Work: A Non-Sexist Approach* (Paoli, PA: The Instructo Corp., n.d.); *Non-Sexist Community Careers for the Flannel Board* (Paoli, PA: The Instructo Corp., n.d.); *Our Helpers: 12 Play People in the Community* (Springfield Mass.: Milton Bradley Company, 1974).

Springboard Lesson 2 is based on an analysis using the language criterion. The lesson has been planned for intermediate/middle school grades. The description of language used in the textbooks is real. The three samples mirror the magnitude of the language problem that publishers are now attempting to correct.

SPRINGBOARD LESSON 2

Intermediate/Middle School—Language

Description:

A powerful and persistent pattern exists in the English language that draws attention to males in the written word. The universality of this pattern is perpetuated in this textbook. The early pages of the book use masculine nouns and pronouns such as "man," "he," "him," and "his" to describe the hypothetical person. These words are used generically a total of 13 times in the three pages of sample 1. In sample 2, 12 masculine nouns and pronouns are used a total of 35 times. The third sample used eight nouns and pronouns 25 times to describe the persons involved in a political system. The three sections of the textbook do not use a single female noun or pronoun while using 16 different male-oriented words. Is the social studies textbook indicating that historical and social phenomena occur only for men? Women do not have an identity in the three samples, except as they are subsumed to men by language.

Objective:

The students will write reports that focus on the use of nonsexist language to record human phenomena in social studies.

Activities:

1. The students might write a report regarding the role of anthropologists in the twentieth century. The purpose of the report would be to focus on the use of language that is neither masculine nor feminine. Physical anthropologists could be discussed from the viewpoint of their roles in the clothing industry. Paleontologists could be examined in relation to their efforts to document the physical changes in humans over the centuries.
2. Have the students design crossword puzzle games in small groups. They would need to generate their own definitions and words. The basic rule would be that each word used in the puzzle would have to reflect a corrected sexist definition. The "across" words might deal with male stereotypes while the "down" words might deal with female stereotypes.
3. The students might write a report on one of the fields in which women hold positions, such as business, education, or government. Employment brochures could be examined to see how recent publications reflect nonsexist or sexist presentation of females and males; for examples, students study *man's* history (cue)—*human* (answer).

Information Source:

Lakoff, Robin. *Language and Woman's Place.* New York: Harper & Row, 1975.

Springboard Lesson 3 looks at the role of women as main characters in response to the stereotypes portrayed in a textbook on government. This lesson has been prepared for the secondary social studies classroom. The textbook, although sexist, has been used in many classrooms during the decade of the 1970s.

SPRINGBOARD LESSON 3

Secondary—Role

Description:

The impression is left that men have dominated American government for the entire period of the history of the United States. However, there have been significant roles played by women as elected officials, as advisors, and as change agents. These roles have been ignored by this textbook. The index of the textbook identifies more than 100 people by name. Only three are women. Not only are women ignored as main characters in the textbook, they are not recognized for any role in American government. The masculine subsuming language in the text reinforces the male image associated with the pronoun "he." A discussion of the ambassador to the United Nations, in the position's generic sense, is always followed by the pronoun "he." In one section of the textbook, fewer than 10 pictures and illustrations are identifiable as women; more than 100 can be identified as men. Women are underrepresented and misrepresented in the textbook.

Objective:

The students will identify significant persons and events associated with American government that reflect the roles that women have had in the formation and growth of our system of government.

Activities:

1. The students could research the history of the United States to identify women who have had a role in our government. One research topic could be Voting. Another could be Interest Groups. A pageant could be planned that would trace the history of voting or of interest groups from the Colonial period to the present. Nonsexist themes could characterize the pageant.
2. Biographical sketches could be prepared on women who have served in the government of the United States. This could be done at the local, county, state, and federal levels. Special attention could be given to laws that the person might have been responsible for during a specific term of office.
3. Women in various roles in government (at all levels) could be interviewed by class members. For those unavailable to the class for an interview, letters with a limited number of questions could be sent. The students could compile a list of responses and explanations under headings such as Issues, Successes, and Unresolved Problems.

Information Source:

Macleod, J.S., and Silverman, S.T. *"You Won't Do": What Textbooks on U.S. History Teach High School Girls.* Pittsburgh, PA: KNOW, Inc., 1973.

CONCLUDING COMMENTS

Progress has been made in textbooks published recently to correct sex stereotypes. Nevertheless, glaring examples of stereotypes still exist when the books are examined with the full spectrum of overt and covert instances of sexism.

There are some good examples of efforts to eliminate sexism available to social studies teachers. One of the best is a biology textbook published in 1978.[10] The editor and publisher made a conscious effort to eliminate sexism in language, occupations, and illustrations. The exemplary aspect of the book concerns in-depth presentations of careers in biology. Ratios were consistently 1 to 1. One shortcoming, however, was the 4 to 1 ratio for male to female minority persons in illustrations. The mi-

---

[10]N. L. Haynes (Editor), *Biological Science: An Ecological Approach*, 4th Edition (Chicago: Rand McNally, 1978).

nority female has a double burden of differential treatment to bear—race and sex. Guidelines for the nonsexist treatment of females and males are available from associations such as the American Psychological Association and the National Council of Teachers of English and from publishers such as McGraw-Hill and Macmillan. These guidelines are useful in getting ideas for Springboard Lesson activities.

Textbooks are an important part of the social studies program in most schools. They will continue to be present in the future. Classroom teachers have a responsibility to correct the sex-role stereotypes when possible. They should also become actively involved in exerting pressure to correct negative images. Until the textbooks are changed, they will continue to function as adverse stimuli in the formation of students' knowledge and values concerning others and—equally important—themselves.

Chapter 6

Correcting Ethnic Stereotypes in Textbooks

William E. Patton

The treatment most ethnic groups have received in many textbooks does not meet the minimum requirements needed to teach these groups' values and traditions. The uniqueness that characterizes the richness of each ethnic group is lost in the predominantly Anglo-American nature of many social studies textbooks. The purpose of this chapter is to focus on the need for students' broad exposure in the social studies classroom to a variety of ethnic groups. James Banks summarizes the value of such a purpose:

> ... each curriculum should focus on a range of groups that differ in their racial characteristics, cultural experiences, languages, histories, values, and current problems. By studying a wide range of ethnic groups, students will be able to derive valid comparative generalizations about the nature of ethnicity in American society.[1]

ETHNICALLY-BIASED TEXTBOOKS

The term "biased" rather than "racist" will be used in this chapter. Racism reflects a prejudice concerning a subset of ethnic groups. Race is only one criterion that can be used to establish the identity of an ethnic group. Language, cultural heritage, and behavior patterns are three additional criteria. A component of racist behavior, which is the differential treatment of a person or group by another person or group because of a racial identity, will be used to describe direct and indirect bias toward ethnic groups. It is the differential treatment of some minority ethnic groups that has resulted in their limited exposure or complete absence in social studies textbooks.

[1]J. A. Banks, *Teaching Strategies for Ethnic Studies*, 2nd. Edition (Boston: Allyn and Bacon, 1979), p. 12.

Differential Treatment

The differential treatment received by ethnic groups in many social studies textbooks is one form of institutional bias. The fact of this bias has been documented in a number of studies. Two investigations sponsored by the Anti-Defamation League of B'nai B'rith examined 48 secondary social studies textbooks published between 1952 and 1961[2] and a second group of 45 published between 1963 and 1971.[3] In the decade between the two studies, it was found that the treatment of Blacks and Native Americans had improved, but that reporting on other groups such as Jewish Americans, Asian Americans, and Hispanics was weak at best. One report stated, "in social studies textbooks, the Mexican American has replaced the Black . . . as the 'invisible American.' Puerto Ricans fare only slightly better."[4] Sloan conducted studies during the 1960s and early 1970s that focused on Blacks in American history textbooks.[5] Blacks and other ethnic groups were the focus of attention of other studies dealing with elementary social studies textbooks.[6] More recently, the Council on Interracial Books for Children published a study that validated many of the criticisms made by earlier studies.[7] The problem of bias toward a number of ethnic groups continues in social studies textbooks.

The pessimistic tone in the review of differential treatment does not mean that pos-
itive changes have not been initiated by authors and publishers. Today ethnic groups are visible in textbooks. Indeed, the proportion of minority ethnic persons discussed and illustrated in an increasing number of primary-grade texts is in excess of the actual ratio between minorities and majority found in our society. Similarly, secondary United States history books picture various aspects of ethnic traditions and roles. An example is the involvement of Black Americans in this country's wars. Pictures of Black units in the Civil War, on the western frontier, in Cuba, and in World War I are displayed. The narratives may not elaborate on the role of Black units, but their involvement is portrayed. The presence of specific personalities has also risen significantly. People representing historic and contemporary dimensions of ethnic groups are included. Powhatan and Sitting Bull, and Crispus Attucks and Frances Harper, as well as many others from a variety of ethnic groups, are being included in narratives. The fact of their inclusion in the textbooks is evidence of change.

Shortcomings in recent efforts to publish less biased social studies textbooks can still be identified. First, increasing the number of ethnics in pictures gives a sense of their personhood, but it does little to clarify their unique values and other cultural elements. Pictures are only one way of providing positive role models and building pride in ethnic differences. The textbook narrative must bring these elements into focus in a social and historical context. Second, many textbooks have added discussions of ethnics by giving details in special accounts of certain individuals or by inserting, almost as an addendum, descriptions of ethnic groups. A discussion in a United States history textbook of the problems faced by Mexican Americans during the 1970s without equal attention given to them during other periods of American history is little more than tokenism. Anglo-American values and traditions are fully integrated in most textbooks. Individuals may disagree on interpretations, but at least information is in the books. Classroom teachers should do the same for other ethnic groups. Many ethnics would wel-

[2]L. Marcus, *The Treatment of Minorities in Secondary School Textbooks* (New York: Anti-Defamation League of B'nai B'rith, 1961).

[3]M. B. Kane, *Minorities in Textbooks: A Study of Their Treatment in Social Studies Texts* (Chicago: Quadrangle Books, 1970).

[4]*Ibid.*, p. 141.

[5]For example, I. Sloan, *The Negro in Modern American History Textbooks* (Chicago: American Federation of Teachers, 1966).

[6]W. W. Joyce, "Minorities in Primary-Grade Social Studies Textbooks: A Progress Report," *Social Education* (March 1973), pp. 218–233; R. C. Turner and J. A. Dewar, "Black History in Selected American History Textbooks," *Educational Leadership* (February 1973), pp. 441–444.

[7]The Council on Interracial Books for Children, *Stereotypes, Distortions and Omissions in U.S. History Textbooks* (New York: The Council, 1977).

come the opportunity to discuss the interpretations of the information detailed in an integrated textbook which reflects their individual groups as elements present in the mainstream of our pluralistic society. Social studies textbooks still have progress to make before ethnic studies are fully integrated.

Although some of the criteria for analyzing and criticizing social studies textbooks' treatment of ethnic groups have changed over the last two decades, a number of criteria are generally acceptable. The value of the criteria listed below is their use in identifying starting points for strengthening ethnic images through springboard lessons.

Do textbooks and curricular materials:

1. characterize the pluralistic nature of the United States in visuals *and* narrative?
2. illustrate hypothetical ethnic individuals and/or families with photographs to depict them accurately?
3. avoid presenting stereotypes of ethnics in their historic and contemporary roles?
4. present members of ethnic groups as outstanding individuals and in affiliated relationships as members of groups?
5. reflect the positive as well as the negative dimensions of an ethnic group's participation in American society?
6. portray the significant and representative aspects of ethnic groups' traditions and values?
7. present the most accurate and up-to-date information available from scholars on all ethnic groups?

Documenting Differential Treatment

This section will focus on three specific analytical techniques for applying the above criteria to social studies textbooks. Specifically, they will deal with tokenism, omissions, and balance. *Tokenism* can take at least two forms in textbooks. First, representatives of ethnic groups can be shown in photographs or paintings but not discussed in the narrative. Second, ethnics can be presented as individuals but without any discussion of ethnics in affiliated or group settings, particularly group settings de-

voted to action. How often is the Black Caucus or Hispanic Caucus discussed as action-oriented organizations for minority members of Congress? When textbooks present representatives in pictures or narrative without discussion or elaboration of their roles, the "exposure" is superficial and warrants the label of tokenism. Table 1 can be used to document tokenism in social studies textbooks. (See p. 52.)

Use of Table 1 with primary-grade textbooks that do not have an index will require study of pictures and narrative. Textbooks in higher grades can be analyzed by examining the index as a first step to identify representatives of minority ethnic groups. The names would be entered in the first column. For some primary-grade textbooks the names may be fictional. The page numbers are also recorded. The content is then examined for pictures, discussion, and the nature of the person's affiliation. It is not necessary for every person to receive a "yes" mark in columns two, three, and four. However, a final tally of 80% "yes" under pictures, 40% "yes" for discussion in the narrative, and 100% "no" for affiliations would provide evidence of tokenism. Ethnic groups can also be entered in the first column and a similar analysis of the content can be made. A good check would involve repeating the process with Anglo-American males, as individuals and in groups, depicted in the textbook. (Majority females suffer the same discrimination as minority ethnics.) A higher percentage of "yes" responses in each column would positively establish differential treatment if the same percentage were not received by minority ethnics.

Omissions, as the second analysis criterion, are particularly significant in history books. The most common form is the omission of decades or even of centuries in the lives of ethnic groups. Do Jews disappear about the time of Jesus Christ's crucifixion and reappear with the formation of the modern state of Israel in 1948? Are Japanese Americans mentioned for the last time as war internees during World War II? Are Afro-Americans discussed in any context prior to the early 1600s? Is Mansa Musa and the great Mali Empire presented in the

Table 1

Criterion One: **Are representatives of ethnic minorities presented disproportionately in pictures without discussion and affiliated relationships?**

Name(s)	Picture		Narrative		Affiliated	
	Yes	No	Yes	No	Yes	No
1.	—	—	—	—	—	—
2.	—	—	—	—	—	—
3.	—	—	—	—	—	—
4.	—	—	—	—	—	—
5.	—	—	—	—	—	—
6.	—	—	—	—	—	—
7.	—	—	—	—	—	—
8.	—	—	—	—	—	—
9.	—	—	—	—	—	—
10.	—	—	—	—	—	—
11.	—	—	—	—	—	—
12.	—	—	—	—	—	—
13.	—	—	—	—	—	—
14.	—	—	—	—	—	—
15.	—	—	—	—	—	—
16.	—	—	—	—	—	—
17.	—	—	—	—	—	—
	% Yes __		% Yes __		% Yes __	

world history textbooks? The list of questions could go on at length. Table 2 allows a teacher to examine history textbooks for omissions. The first step in using the analysis sheet is identifying the critical events in the history of ethnic groups. The Ethnic Heritage Projects of the New Jersey Education Association and National Education Association have produced an excellent document which reviews dates and events in the lives of many ethnic groups.[8] The second edition of James Banks' useful book, *Teaching Strategies for Ethnic Studies,* also includes a chronological overview of events of significance to ethnics and their presence in the United States and world.[9] Both of these publications provide bibliographies on individual ethnic groups, including European Americans. (See p. 54.)

Once the desired events are listed in the first column, the table of contents, index, and body of the textbook are checked for evidence of each entry. The presence or absence of material is recorded in the second and third columns. The fourth column can be used to indicate the substance of the discussion regarding the values and/or feelings of ethnics. An understanding of ethnic groups comes through exposure to their presence *and* their feelings. Bigotry and false images are more easily countered when the intellectual and emotional character of people is communicated. A separate table can be used for each ethnic group or category.

No single social studies textbook can possibly present every major event for every ethnic group in the United States. What, then, is the minimal level of treatment that can be recorded on the table without labeling the textbook inadequate? No precise answer can be given in quantitative terms. One possibility involves two questions: Did the event have a significant impact on the pluralistic nature of the United States or world? And were the val-

ues and traditions of the ethnic group significantly influenced by the event? An affirmative answer to either question might require an event's presence in a social studies textbook. Teachers need to avoid selecting only those events that represent a material contribution.

The last criterion for analyzing a textbook is *balance.* When a social studies textbook presents a composite picture of events that make up the past, present, and future for ethnic groups and which reflects the positive and negative dimensions of roles, traditions, and values, it will have balance. A textbook that meets the requirements of this criterion will have achieved maturity and will become an invaluable resource for integrating ethnic studies into the school curriculum. Table 3. (see p. 55) displays the analysis structure. Events presented in the textbook will be recorded on Table 2. The teacher will transfer these to Table 3 and record the page numbers in the first column. The pictures are examined and the narrative is read for evidence of negative and positive information. The teacher needs to be very aware of ethnocentrism at this point. However, teachers should not rely on their own feelings of what is negative and what is positive. Rather, they should heighten their awareness of ethnic groups through study and dialogue. Initial impressions should be checked carefully to avoid incorrect or inappropriate classifications in columns two and three. Older students using these tables to check their textbooks could treat their first impressions as hypotheses and gather new information to validate or invalidate these impressions.

All three tables reflect a progressive analysis of social studies textbooks. The first examines the superficial aspects of content dealing with ethnics, while the last makes it possible to examine the meaning of the content. Information from the tables will document the presence or absence of differential treatment of ethnic groups.

IMPROVING ETHNIC IMAGES

The basic rationale for examining social studies textbooks for examples of biased treatment of ethnic groups is tied to a belief

---

[8]New Jersey Education Association and National Education Association, *Roots of America: A Multiethnic Curriculum Resource Guide for 7th, 8th, and 9th Grade Social Studies Teachers* (Washington, D.C.: National Education Association, 1975).

[9]Banks, *Teaching Strategies for Ethnic Studies.*

Table 2

Criterion Two: **Are significant events from an ethnic group's heritage—events that have influenced both that group and our pluralistic country/world—omitted in the textbook?**

Event	Picture		Narrative		Values/Feelings	
	Yes	No	Yes	No	Yes	No
1.	—	—	—	—	—	—
2.	—	—	—	—	—	—
3.	—	—	—	—	—	—
4.	—	—	—	—	—	—
5.	—	—	—	—	—	—
6.	—	—	—	—	—	—
7.	—	—	—	—	—	—
8.	—	—	—	—	—	—
9.	—	—	—	—	—	—
10.	—	—	—	—	—	—
11.	—	—	—	—	—	—
12.	—	—	—	—	—	—
13.	—	—	—	—	—	—
14.	—	—	—	—	—	—
15.	—	—	—	—	—	—

Table 3

Criterion Three: **Do the events in the textbook communicate positive as well as negative
information about an ethnic group?**

Narrative/Picture Element	Positive		Negative	
	Yes	No	Yes	No
1.	—	—	—	—
2.	—	—	—	—
3.	—	—	—	—
4.	—	—	—	—
5.	—	—	—	—
6.	—	—	—	—
7.	—	—	—	—
8.	—	—	—	—
9.	—	—	—	—
10.	—	—	—	—
11.	—	—	—	—
12.	—	—	—	—
13.	—	—	—	—
14.	—	—	—	—
15.	—	—	—	—
16.	—	—	—	—

in the pluralistic nature of the American culture. Going one step further in the process of strengthening ethnic images involves correcting the biased images. In many cases it means an acceptance of the differences within and between people of different ethnic backgrounds. C. A. Grant expressed a view that is central to a belief in the need for strengthening images:

> . . . all people must be accorded *respect*, regardless of their social, ethnic, religious, and cultural backgrounds. Unless we respect and cultivate the differences among all people and give more equal weight to various kinds of gifts than we now do, we shall produce a deadening uniformity.[10]

The respect that should be shown to all people, notwithstanding their ethnic identity, can develop through the actions of teachers in their classrooms as they improve ethnic images.

General Approaches for Correcting Images

One approach involves students in identifying aspects of minority ethnic input into the social, economic, and political life of the United States and the world. Much emphasis has been placed on the contributions made by individuals representing ethnic groups. In some instances, however, the tone of the words is so patronizing that a reader may wonder how someone with "this background" could possibly do anything. The contributions are usually discussed in isolation and apart from the larger societal setting in which they occurred. Is the poetry of Frances Harper and Paul Laurence Dunbar presented as part of the mainstream of American literature? Teachers and students must go beyond the "contribution" theme which too often treats individuals as isolated phenomena. To picture life for Native Americans on the plains, a teacher can use the paintings of

Standing Bear, an Oglala Sioux, as well as those done by Remington. Ethnic vitality in the development of our pluralistic society is an actuality, not in isolation, but in concert with all ethnic groups.

A second approach to correcting ethnic images builds on the previous one. A practice for dealing with ethnic images and contributions involves special days or weeks in the social studies curriculum. A Black history week, a day for the Chinese New Year, and traditional Jewish food for Hanukkah are some examples. The shortcoming of this practice is its isolationist character. Differences are emphasized; the similarities with other ethnic groups are given little attention or ignored. Teachers and students must integrate information at all levels—such as contributions, life styles, and events—into the regular social studies curriculum. When a textbook does not deal with an important aspect of ethnic life, that aspect should be included at an appropriate point in the curriculum. Many pages in a social studies textbook may be devoted to the reasons why Anglo-Americans emigrated from their native land. Is similar treatment given to Italian Americans or Cuban Americans who left their lands? The different waves of immigrants are understood only as the various groups' motivations are examined. Isolated study, therefore, does not encourage general understanding. The efforts of Cesar Chavez and many other Chicanos to gain a living wage and the right to organize and negotiate contracts are one aspect of the long history of the labor movement in the United States. Without such facts being integrated into the central theme of the social studies textbook or curriculum, differences may be stressed at the expense of differences *and* similarities. Both must be understood in relation to ethnic groups. The integration of ethnic studies does not mean that unique features are to be absorbed. They should be stressed to develop cross-ethnic competencies in students.

These competencies are the central thrust of the third approach to correcting ethnic images. The language of cross-ethnic understanding or competency has usually referred to international studies. When

---

[10]C. A. Grant (Editor), "Anthropological Foundations of Education That Is Multicultural," in C. A. Grant (Editor), *Multicultural Education: Commitments, Issues, and Applications* (Washington, D.C.: Association for Supervision and Curriculum Development, 1977), p. 38.

examined in relation to the development of ethnic studies, it draws on a tradition which developed more than 30 years ago with studies and discussions of intergroup relations.[11] All individuals, regardless of their ethnic affiliations, need to understand the traditions and values of other ethnic groups. A history that is predominantly Hispanic creates limitations for learners in the same way as one that reflects an Anglo-American bias. Stereotypes can be neutralized when a knowledge and understanding of the diverse ethnic elements are learned in the social studies classroom. This can be accomplished when teachers organize learning experiences that foster cross-ethnic competencies.

Space will not be devoted to more specific techniques for strengthening ethnic im-

ages other than the Springboard Lessons. Resources currently available to teachers are extensive. The footnotes in this chapter are one source of information. Another is a bibliography with nearly 100 citations to help teachers.[12] The result of contact with even a limited number of these resources will be a wealth of specific techniques for supplementing textbooks in order to accomplish the goals of ethnic studies.

SPRINGBOARD LESSONS

Each Springboard Lesson has been designed to reflect the application of the general approaches to strengthening ethnic images in our pluralistic society. Students will discover through each of the lessons that ethnic groups do have unique cultural features, such as language, food, and values. In the midst of differences, however, they will be able to identify many similarities. Students will be able to identify with many elements of our pluralistic society because of events and feelings that draw people together. These seeds of understanding are important to develop cross-ethnic competencies within students. (**Springboard Lessons appear on pp. 58–60.**)

---

[11]Committee on the Study of Teaching Materials in Intergroup Relations, *Intergroup Relations in Teaching Materials* (Washington, D.C.: American Council on Education, 1949).

[12]M. Dunfee, "Resources for Educators," in M. Dunfee (Editor), *Eliminating Ethnic Bias in Instructional Materials: Comment and Bibliography* (Washington, D.C.: Association for Supervision and Curriculum Development, 1974), pp. 35–41.

Springboard Lesson 1 is designed to bring primary-grade students into direct contact with tangible elements of different ethnic groups. These will include foods and places of origin. The lesson can be used to reinforce critical thinking skills (drawing conclusions) and map skills (location). One variation of the first activity might be implemented in an ethnically homogeneous community or school. The students could identify the ethnic/cultural origin of foods that have become acceptable parts of the American culture; e.g., wonton, pancake, and shish kebab. The foods in both cases could be prepared and sampled.

SPRINGBOARD LESSON 1

Primary—Pictures with Discussion

Description:

Primary-grade social studies textbooks are often restricted in their ability to use narrative. The younger students need concrete references to deal with facts, concepts, and feelings. Sometimes the narrative is limited to questions that direct students' attention to the visuals in the textbook. Under these conditions information about ethnic groups is usually communicated through the visuals. The different ethnic groups are named and questions are asked about attributes of the identifiable characteristics in the pictures. An occasional declarative sentence may be included. When organizing centers are concepts such as climate or work, ethnicity is a secondary concern—if it is any concern at all. Young students' awareness of ethnic groups, however, comes from television and their own experiences in school and the neighborhood. Additional activities need to be planned to supplement the visuals in textbooks and children's experiences outside the classroom.

Objective:

The students will identify features of their home, school, and community environment that reflect ethnic diversity.

Activities:

1. Using food as the organizing center, have the students bring examples (pictures) of their favorite dish or dessert. Parents should be informed to elicit their cooperation. Encouragement should be given to have students bring something that reflects their ethnic backgrounds. Using a data retrieval chart, students could place the pictures and words on the chart in rows next to the ethnic description:

Ethnic Group	Picture	Name
Greek		Baklava
Mexican		Ojaldrados

   The teacher would direct questions to the students to reach conclusions about similarities and differences in foods. Word-attack skills could be used to help them pronounce the names. The same process could be done with ethnic holidays, festivals, or native clothing.
2. Have students obtain a family picture or use a student's school picture. After the students have a picture and information on their ethnic backgrounds, use a map of the world and have the students create a bulletin board with their pictures attached to a country (Japan—Tokyo) or state (North Dakota) with yarn and pins. The pictures in the margin of the map would track to the location of origin by the yarn. Questions could be asked about patterns of origin and students' backgrounds.

Information Source:

Tiedt, P. L. and I. M. Tiedt. *Multicultural Teaching: A Handbook of Activities, Information, and Resources.* Boston: Allyn and Bacon, 1979.

Springboard Lesson 2 is structured to deal with one aspect of Native American history that is not given complete coverage in United States history textbooks. Usually the truth, from the Native American perspective, regarding the Removal Act of 1830 and the Trail of Tears is not detailed in textbooks. Upper elementary and lower junior high school students can read primary sources (information gathering) and compare actual accounts with textbook coverage (evaluation). The horror of these events for Native Americans can become an intellectual and emotional experience for students when they are compared to more recent inhumane actions by people in different parts of the world.

SPRINGBOARD LESSON 2

Intermediate/Middle School—Omissions

Description:

Many intermediate/middle school United States history books now include a section on the Indian Removal Program. Some actions by our government in the early decades of the 1800s rank high on the list of overt acts of inhumanity. Some social studies textbooks present a discussion of the general events associated with the background to and the circumstances surrounding the Trail of Tears. Missing, however, are two important dimensions of the entire sequence for the Cherokee Nation. First, the great discrepancy between the cultural advances of the Cherokees and the relative "backwardness" of the Whites living to the east of these Native Americans is either ignored or downplayed. Second, the consistent disregard for territorial claims and Native Americans' lives by the government in Washington, D.C. and by the troops before and during the march to the lands west of the Mississippi is treated in an unrealistic manner. Thousands lost their lives due to brutality, starvation, and exposure. Too much of the Cherokee story is omitted from textbooks.

Objective:

The students will comprehend the events surrounding the destruction of the Cherokee Nation and the Trail of Tears as viewed by the Cherokees and others.

Activities:

1. Provide excerpts for students from a variety of sources regarding the Trail of Tears, its background, and its aftermath; e.g., Cherokee accounts, de Tocqueville's account (Choctaw), President Van Buren's report to Congress, and accounts of General Scott's actions. Sequoya's efforts could be discussed also. Students should list at least five myths stated by the government and its representatives. For each myth a counterpoint statement should be prepared from other sources. What parallels to the Cherokee situation have existed in the twentieth century? (Southeast Asia's Boat People, Nazi Death Camps, Bataan Death March.)

2. From the accounts and descriptions of the Trail of Tears, have the students prepare a bulletin board or wall mural portraying the events before, during, and after the march. The central focus might be a map showing the original land of the Cherokee Nation and the path of the march to what is today Oklahoma. Specific information could be placed at different points on the map. Sequoya in his homeland, the Supreme Court decision in favor of the Cherokees, the Removal Act, and temperatures along the trail during the winter of 1838–39 are some examples.

Information Sources:

Farb, P. *Man's Rise to Civilization as Shown by the Indians of North America from Primeval Times to the Coming of the Industrial State.* New York: Dutton, 1968.

Washburn, W. E. *The Indian in America.* New York: Harper & Row, 1975.

Springboard Lesson 3 examines another aspect of United States history. The role and values of Harriet Tubman as an active abolitionist are presented in a limited way in some textbooks. Her actions as viewed by many southerners and some more peaceful northerners may not be treated positively. High school students can examine the negative and positive views (analysis) toward her and formulate their own positions (valuing). The springboard activities provide opportunities for writing, discussion, and role playing. Harriet Tubman stands with many Black Americans as an ardent abolitionist who took direct action.

SPRINGBOARD LESSON 3

Secondary—Positive and Negative Portrayal

Description:

A limited discussion of the underground railroad as a system established and maintained by abolitionists and sympathizers during the pre-Civil War period concerns minority ethnic-group involvement. Credit is given to a number of men and to two women—the Grimké sisters—as principal abolitionists. Black Americans involved in the antislavery movement during pre-Civil War days are mentioned briefly and in most cases only by name. One Black in particular, Harriet Tubman, had a principal role as an abolitionist and as a "conductor" on the underground railroad system. With her basic value expressed in the motto "You will be free or die" and her outstanding organizational capabilities, Harriet Tubman made many trips into the South before and during the Civil War to free slaves.

Objective:

The students will describe the role and values of Harriet Tubman as an abolitionist and as an activist in the underground railroad system.

Activities:

1. The students might write an editorial that might have been published, hypothetically, in the antislavery magazine *The Liberator*, summarizing the values and the actions of Harriet Tubman.
2. The students might write a play involving two characters—Harriet Tubman and a slave fleeing from the South. The play would center on Harriet Tubman's effective style and central values during a segment of the journey north.
3. The students might prepare a wall map showing the central route followed during Harriet Tubman's many trips to and from the south. "Wanted" posters might be prepared for attachment to the southern portion of the map. The posters would present the negative view of her efforts. They would reflect a slaveowner's perceptions of the abolitionist. Newspaper clippings could be prepared and attached to the northern portion of the map. These clippings might summarize the thoughts of a former slave freed by Harriet Tubman.

Information Sources:

Ladner, J. A. "The Women; Conditions of Slavery Laid the Foundation for Their Liberation." *Ebony*, August 1975, *30*, p. 77.

Petry, A. *Harriet Tubman: Conductor on the Underground Railroad.* New York: Washington Square Press, 1955.

Chapter 7

The Study of Textbooks and Schoolbooks: A Selective Bibliography

Jean Dresden Grambs

Twelve years ago two colleagues and I collected all of the items we could find which addressed the question of textbook content.[1] We included published as well as unpublished material, but the list was not especially long. If one does not count the unpublished material, we could only locate 164 books, articles, or monographs which discussed textbook content.

The bibliography which follows in this Bulletin is far different. For one thing, the sheer number of items has forced the omission of unpublished studies. The researcher who wishes to obtain a true canvass of the field should look to dissertation abstracts and nonpublished material in the ERIC data base.

How can we account for the vast increase in items? In 1968 there were only the beginnings of awareness of the damage which might occur to the perceptions students had of reality if their textbooks presented a biased picture. Today we are increasingly sensitive to the impact upon the reader which can result from bias in word usage, picture selection, or omission of data. The reviewers of textbooks are looking at bias in presentation of racial groups, and they are also studying the sexist bias in texts. Some researchers are concerned with ideological bias. Studies of texts

which were, in 1968, primarily focused on language arts and social studies books, now also occur in all fields—mathematics, biology, economics, home economics, vocational education—and at both school and college levels.

The following bibliography is not comprehensive; lack of time and assistance made it impossible to comb all of the possible sources. Within these constraints, however, the listing is relatively complete.

Some interesting observations can be made about the list: None of the studies, for example, reports on the presentation of the teacher in school textbooks. There are few studies which appear to analyze the changing view of men (if there has been one) to parallel the efforts to change the way women are presented. Children, as presented in texts and schoolbooks, are not studied with attention to whether or not they are seen as valued and self-directing individuals experiencing opportunities to make informed choices. There are relatively few trend studies. There are other lacunae which the researcher will find interesting, and which call out for studious investigation. As the pre-eminent educator, the textbook deserves continued serious analysis and study.

JEAN DRESDEN GRAMBS is Professor of Human Development at the University of Maryland at College Park.

[1]Jean Dresden Grambs, Loretta Golden, and Barbara Finkelstein, "A Bibliography of Research and Commentary on Textbooks and School Books," *Social Education*, March 1969, *33*, pp. 331–336.

Historical Analysis: Books and Monographs

Altschal, Charles. *The American Revolution in Our School Books*. New York: George H. Doran Co., 1917.

American Council on Education. *Intergroup Relations in Teaching Materials*. Washington, D.C.: American Council on Education, 1949.

Barry, F. U. A. *A Century of Children's Books*. New York: Doran, 1932.

Cronbach, Lee J. (ed.). *Text Materials in Modern Education*. Urban, Ill., University of Illinois Press, 1975.

Elson, Ruth Miller. *Guardians of Tradition: American Schoolbooks of the Nineteenth Century*. Lincoln: University of Nebraska Press, 1972.

Foff, Arthur. "The Teacher as Hero." In *Readings in Education*, edited by Arthur Foff and Jean D. Grambs, pp. 19–21. New York: Harper & Row, Publishers, 1956.

Hardy, G. E. P. *Literature for Children*. New York: Scribner's, 1892.

Hazlitt, W. Carey. *Schools, Schoolbooks and Schoolmasters*. New York: Stetchert and Co., 2nd edition, 1905.

Heartman, Charles. *The New England Primer Prior to 1830*. New York: Privately Printed, 1916.

James, Philip. *Children's Books of Yesterday*. London: The Studio Publications, 1933.

Johnson, Clifton. *Old Time Schools and Schoolbooks*. New York: Dover Publishing Co., 1963 (reprint of 1904 ed.).

Keiser, Albert. *The Indian in American Literature*. New York: Oxford University Press, 1933.

Kiefer, Monica. *American Children Through Their Books—1790–1835*. Philadelphia: University of Pennsylvania Press, 1948.

Livermore, George. *The Origin, History, and Character of the New England Primer*. New York: Privately Printed, 1915.

Martin, Helen. *Nationalism in Children's Literature*. Chicago: University of Chicago Press, 1934.

Meigs, Cornelia, Anne Eaton, Elizabeth Nesbitt, and Ruth H. Viguers. *A Critical History of Children's Literature*. New York: Macmillan, 1953.

Merriweather, Colyer. *Our Colonial Curriculum 1607–1776*. Washington, D.C.: Capitol Publishing Co., 1907.

Minnich, Harvey C. *William Holmes McGuffey and His Readers*. New York: American Book Co., 1936.

Mosier, Richard D. *Making the American Mind: Social and Moral Ideas in the McGuffey Readers*. New York: King's Crown Press, Columbia University, 1947.

National Society for the Study of Education. *The Text Book in American Education*, Thirtieth Yearbook, Part II. Chicago: University of Chicago Press, 1931.

Peacock, Fletcher and James Edmonston. *A Study of National History Textbooks Used in the Schools of Canada and the United States*, Canada-United States Committee on Education. Washington, D.C.: American Council on Education, 1949.

Pierce, Bessie. *Civic Attitudes in American Textbooks*. Chicago: University of Chicago Press, 1930.

Quillen, I. James. *Textbook Improvement and International Understanding*. American Council on Education, 1948.

Root, Merrill E. *Brainwashing in the High Schools*. New York: The Devin-Adair Co., 1958.

Roselle, Daniel. *Samuel Griswold Goodrich: Creator of Peter Parley*. New York: State University of New York Press, 1968.

Rosenbach, A. S. W. *Early American Children's Books*. Portland: Southworth Press, 1933.

Schlesinger, Arthur. *Learning How to Behave: A Historical Study of American Etiquette Books*. New York: Macmillan Co., 1946.

Shepard, Jon P. *The Treatment of Characters in Popular Children's Fiction*. Berkeley: University of California Press, 1958.

Smith, Dora V. *Fifty Years of Children's Books: 1910–1960*. Champaign, Ill.: National Council of Teachers of English, 1963.

Spieseke, Alice Winifred. *The First Textbooks in American History, and Their Compiler, John M'Culloch*. New York: Teachers College, Columbia University, 1938.

Stewart, Maxwell. *Prejudice in Textbooks*. New York: Public Affairs Pamphlets, 1960.

Sunley, Robert. "Early Nineteenth-Century American Literature on Child Rearing." In *Childhood in Contemporary Cultures*, edited by Margaret Mead and Martha Wolfenstein. Chicago: University of Chicago Press, 1955, 150–167.

Vail, Henry H. *History of McGuffey Readers*. Cleveland: Privately Printed, 1911.

Walworth, Arthur. *School Histories at War—Study of the Treatment of Our Wars in the Secondary School History Books of the United States and in Those of Its Former Enemies*. Cambridge, Mass.: Harvard University Press, 1938.

Weeks, Stephen B. *Confederate Textbooks, 1861–1865*. In Report of The United States Commissioner of Education for 1898–1899. Washington, D.C.: Government Printing Office, 1900.

Wilson, Harold E. *Latin America in School and College Teaching Materials*. Report of the

Committee on the Study of Teaching Materials on Inter-American Subjects. Washington, D.C.: American Council on Education, 1946.

Wiltse, S. E. *The Place of the Story in Early Education*. Boston: Ginn, 1892.

Wines, E. C. *Hints on a System of Popular Education*. Philadelphia: Hogan Thompson, 1838.

Warfel, Henry R. *Noah Webster, Schoolmaster to America*. New York: Macmillan, 1936.

Historical Analysis: Articles

"Are Our Children Learning History with a Slant?" *UNESCO Courier*, May, 1956, 9, 1–3.

Bagenstos, Naida Tushnet. "Social Reconstruction: The Controversy over the Textbooks of Harold Rugg," *Theory and Research in Social Education*, December, 1977, 5, 3, 22–38.

Belock, M. V. "Courtesy Tradition and Early Schoolbooks," *History of Education Quarterly*, Fall, 1968, 8, 306–318.

Belock, M. V. "Noah Webster's Speller and the Way to Success," *Phi Delta Kappan*, October, 1967, 49, 85–87.

Benthul, H. F. "The Textbook: Past and Future," *Curriculum Review*, February, 1978, 17, No. 1, 5–8.

Benthul, H. F. "Trends in Education: The Textbook Past and Future," *Curriculum Review*, May, 1978, 17, No. 2, 89–91.

Black, Isabella. "Race and Unreason: Anti-Negro Opinion in Professional and Scientific Literature since 1954," *Phylon*, Spring, 1965, 26, 65–79.

Blotner, Joseph. *The Political Novel*. Garden City, N.J.: Doubleday & Co., Inc., 1955.

Brown, Ralph. "The American Geographies of Jedidiah Morse," *Annals of the Association of American Geographers*, September, 1941, 30, 145–267.

Burkhardt, R. W. "The Soviet Union in American Textbooks," *Progressive Education*, October 1950, 28, 20–23.

Carpenter, Frederic I. "The Adolescent in American Fiction," *English Journal*, September, 1957, 46, 313–319.

Child, Irvin L., et al. "Children's Textbooks and Personality Development: An Exploration in the Social Psychology of Education," *Psychological Monographs*, 1946, 60, 1–53.

Clyse, Juanita. "What Do Basic Readers Teach about Jobs?" *Elementary School Journal*, May, 1959, 60, 446–460.

Deane, Paul C. "The Persistence of Uncle Tom: An Examination of the Image of the Negro in Children's Fiction Series," *Journal of Negro Education*, April, 1868, 37, 140–145.

Desmond, H. J. "A Grave Omission in American School Histories," *Century Magazine*, October, 1968.

Egger, Rowland. "The Administrative Novel," *American Political Science Review*, June, 1959, 53, 448–455.

Elson, Ruth Miller. "American Schoolbooks and 'Culture' in the Nineteenth Century," *Mississippi Valley Historical Review*, December, 1959, 46, 411–434.

England, Merton J. "The Democratic Faith in American Schoolbooks, 1783–1860," *American Quarterly*, Summer, 1963, 15, 191–199.

England, Merton J. "England and America in the Schoolbooks of the Republic, 1783–1861," *University of Birmingham Historical Journal*, 1963, 9, 92–111.

Evans, Eva Knox. "The Negro in Children's Fiction," *The Publishers Weekly*, October 18, 1941, 140, 650.

Finkelstein, Barbara J. "Choose Your Bias Carefully: Textbooks in the History of American Education," *Educational Studies*, Winter 1974–75, 5, 210–215.

Franklin, John Hope. "Rediscovering Black America: A Historical Roundup," *New York Times Book Review*, September, 1968, 8, 1.

Friedsam, H. J. "Bureaucrats as Heroes," *Social Forces*, March, 1954, 32, 269–274.

Gross, Theodore L. "The Negro in the Literature of Reconstruction," *Phylon*, 1961, 22, 5–14.

Hersey, John. "Why Do Students Bog Down on First 'R'?" *Life*, May 24, 1954, 36, 136–140.

Howe, Irving. *Politics and the Novel*. New York: Horizon Press, 1957.

Johnson, Clifton. "More Quaint Readers," *New England Magazine*, January, 1904. XXIX.

Kelly, R. E. "Writing of Schoolbooks in the Late Eighteenth and Early Nineteenth Centuries," *History of Education Quarterly*, Summer, 1975, 15, 207–211.

Kolmer, E. "McGuffey Readers: Exponents of American Classical Liberalism," *Journal General Education*, Winter, 1975, 27, 309–316.

LeUnes, Arnold. "Contribution to the History of Psychology: XX. A Review of Selected Aspects of Texts in Abnormal Psychology," *Psychological Reports*, December, 1974, 35, 3, 1319–1326.

Morgan, J. W. "Our School Books," *Debow's Review*, XXVII, 1860.

Ohles, John F. "Pioneer Writers of Social Studies Textbooks," *Social Studies*, March, 1979, 67, 66–69.

Plimpton, George A. "The Hornbook and Its Use in America," *Proceedings of American Antiquarian Society*, October, 1961.

"Quackery in American Literature," *Southern Review*, Baltimore, January, 1868.

Reddick, Lawrence D. "Racial Attitudes in American History Textbooks of the South,"

Journal of Negro History, July, 1934, *19*, 225–265.

Reynolds, John C., Jr. "American Textbooks: The First 200 Years—Bicentennial Reflections of Curriculum," *Educational Leadership*, January, 1976, *33*, 88.

Sahli, J. R. "Slavery Issue in Early Geography Textbooks," *History of Education Quarterly*, September, 1963, *3*, 153–158.

Sanford, Charles L. "Classics of American Reform Literature," *American Quarterly*, Fall, 1938, *10*, 295–311.

Saveth, Edward N. "Good Stocks and Lesser Breeds: The Immigrant in American Textbooks," *Commentary*, May, 1949, 7, 494–498.

"School Histories," *Southern Review*, Baltimore, January, 1968, 154–179.

Shankland, Rebecca H. "The McGuffey Readers and Moral Education," *Harvard Educational Review*, Winter, 1961, *31*, 60–72.

Shurter, Robert L. "The Utopian Novel in America, 1888–1900," *South Atlantic Quarterly*, April, 1935, *34*, 137–144.

Suhl, Isabelle. "The Real Doctor Doolittle," *Inter-racial Books for Children*, Spring, Summer, 1969, *2*, 1–2.

Tannenbaum, Abraham. "Family Living in Textbook Town," *Progressive Education*, March, 1954, *31*, 133–141.

Thum, Gladys E. "Bias Against Women in Educational History—A Progaganda Analysis," *Educational Horizons*, Spring, 1977, *55*, 3.

Tyack, David. "Forming the National Character: Paradox in the Educational Thought of the Revolutionary Generation," *Harvard Educational Review*, November, 1963, *34*, 71–78.

Wolfenstein, Martha. "Fun Morality: An Analysis of Recent American Child-Training Literature," *Journal of Social Issues*, 1951, 7, 15–25.

Younker, Donna Lee. "The Moral Philosophy of William Holmes McGuffey," *Educational Forum*, November, 1963, *27*, 71–78.

Zimet, Sara F. "American Elementary Reading Textbooks: A Sociological Review," *Teachers College Record*, January, 1969, *70*, 331–340.

Social Studies: Books and Monographs

American Jewish Committee. *A Study of Racial Bias in Social Studies Textbooks*. Dallas, Texas: American Jewish Committee, Dallas Chapter, 1809 Tower Bldg., Dallas, Texas 75201, 1975, 35 pp.

American Jewish Committee. *Judaism and Jewish History in Instructional Materials*. The Committee, Institute of Human Relations, 165 East 56th Street, NY 10022, 1972, 5 pp.

Arlow, Phyllis and Merle Froschl. "Women in the High School: A Review of U.S. History and English Literature Text." In Carol Ahlum and Jacqueline Fralley (eds.), *High School Feminist Studies*. Old Westbury, New York: Feminist Press, 1976.

Asia in American Textbooks. New York, NY: ASIA Society, May, 1976.

Baronberg, Joan. *Black Representation in Children's Books*. Urban Disadvantaged Series, No. 21, Eric Clearinghouse on the Urban Disadvantaged. New York: Teachers College, Columbia University, May, 1971, 27 pp.

Billington, Ray Allen, et al. *The Historian's Contribution to Anglo-American Misunderstanding: Report of a Committee on National Bias in Anglo-American History Textbooks*. New York: Hobbs, Dorman and Co., Inc., 1966.

Black American Literature Forum (Quarterly). Terre Haute, Ind.: Indiana State University, School of Education.

Britton, Gwyneth and Margaret Lumpkin. *A Consumer's Guide to Sex, Race and Career Bias in Public School Textbooks*. Britton and Associates, Inc., 7549 N.W. Mt. View Drive, Corvallis, Oregon 97330, 77, 438 pp.

Broderick, Dorothy. *Image of the Black in Children's Fiction*. New York: R.R. Bowker, 1973.

Classroom Treatment of the Right to Work: High School History and Government Materials. Fairfax, Va.: National Right to Work Committee, 1977, 38 pp.

Carpenter, Marie E. *The Treatment of the Negro in American History School Textbooks*. Menasha, Wis.: George Banta Publishing Co., 1941.

Coston, Rupert (3d.). *Textbooks and the American Indian*. San Francisco: American Indian Historical Society, Indian Historian Press, 1451 Masonic Avenue, San Francisco 94118, 1970, 296 pp.

Davidson, Donald G., et al. *Economics in the Social Studies Textbooks. An Evaluation of the Economics and the Teaching Strategies in Social Studies Textbooks, Elementary Grades (1–6)*. New York, N.Y.: Joint Council on Economic Education, 1973, 72 pp.

Davidson, Donald G., et al. *Economics in Social Studies Textbooks: An Evaluation of the Economics and the Teaching Strategies in Social Studies Textbooks, Elementary Grades (1–6), Report No. 2*. Bureau of Business and Economic Research College of Business Administration, The University of Iowa, Iowa City, Iowa 52240, 1975, 44 pp.

FitzGerald, Frances. *America Revised*. Boston: An Atlantic Monthly Press Book, Little, Brown and Company, 1979.

Friedlander, Henry. *On the Holocaust: A Critique of the Treatment of the Holocaust in His-*

tory Textbooks, Accompanied by an Annotated Bibliography. Anti-Defamation League of B'nai B'rith, 315 Lexington Ave., NY 10016, 1973, 31 pp.

Griffin, William L. and John Marciano. Teaching the Vietnam War: A Critical Examination of School Texts and an Interpretive Comparative History Utilizing the Pentagon Papers and Other Documents. Montclair, NJ: Allanheld, Osmun & Co., 1980.

Griswald, William J. The Image of the Middle East in Secondary School Textbooks. Middle East Studies Association, Hagop Kevorkian Center for Near Eastern Studies, 50 Washington Square, South, New York University, New York 1003, 1975, 108 pp.

Hall, Susan J. Africa in U.S. Educational Materials: Thirty Problems and Responses. African-American Institute, 833 United Nations Plaza, New York 10017, January, 1977, 65 pp.

Hertz, Martin F. How the Cold War Is Taught: Six American History Textbooks Examined. Georgetown University: Ethics and Public Policy Center, 1211 Connecticut Avenue, N.W. Washington, D.C. 20036, 1978, 82 pp.

Kane, Michael B. Minorities in Textbooks: A Study of Their Treatment in Social Studies Texts. New York: Anti-Defamation League of B'nai B'rith, 315 Lexington Avenue, NY 10015, 1970, 148 pp.

Macleod, Jennifer S. and Sandra Silverman. "You Won't Do": What Textbooks on U.S. Government Teach High School Girls. KNOW, Inc., P.O. Box 86031, Pittsburgh, PA 15221, 1973, 109 pp.

McDairmid, G. and D. Pratt. Teaching Prejudice: A Content Analysis of Social Studies Textbooks Authorized for Use in Ontario. Toronto: The Ontario Institute for Studies in Education, 1971.

Moore, Robert B. Two History Texts: A Study in Contrast. A Study Guide and Lesson Plan. Council on Interracial Books for Children, 1841 Broadway, Room 300, New York, 10023, 1975, 25 pp.

Michigan Social Studies Textbook Study: A Study of Senior High School Government Textbooks. Michigan State Department of Education, Lansing, 1976, 143 pp.

Novak, Michael, et al. Values in an American Government Textbook, Three Appraisals. Ethics and Public Policy Center, 1211 Connecticut Avenue, NW, Washington, D.C. 20036, 1978, 57 pp.

O'Neill, James B. Economics in Social Studies Textbooks. An Evaluation of the Economics and the Teaching Strategies in Eleventh and Twelfth Grade U.S. and World History Textbooks. New York: Joint Council on Economic Education, 1973, 57 pp.

Prida, Dolores, et al. A Feminist View of 100 Books About Puerto Ricans. New York: Council on Interracial Books for Children, 1941 Broadway, N.Y. 10023, 1972.

Prida, Dolores, et al. "The Portrayal of Women in Children's Books on Puerto Rican Themes." In Barbara Yates, Steven Werner, and David Rosen (eds.), We'll Do It Ourselves: Combating Sexism in Education. Lincoln, Nebraska: The Nebraska Curriculum Development Center, University of Nebraska, 1974, 13–32.

Sloan, Irving. The American Labor Movement in Modern History and Government Textbooks. American Federation of Teachers, AFL-CIO, 1012 14th Street, N.W. Washington, D.C 20005, 1974, 53 pp.

Sloan, Irving. The Negro in Modern American History Textbooks, 2nd ed. Chicago: American Federation of Teachers, 1967.

Stereotypes, Distortions and Omissions in U.S. History Textbooks. New York: Council on Interracial Books for Children, 1977, 269 pp.

Watson, George G., Jr., et al. Economics in Social Studies Textbooks. An Evaluation of the Economics and the Teaching Strategies in Social Studies Textbooks, Junior High School (Grades 7–9). New York: Joint Council on Economic Education, 1973, 52 pp.

Weidenaar, Dennis J., et al. Economics in Social Studies Textbooks. An Evaluation of the Economics and the Teaching Strategies in Social Studies Textbooks, High School (Grades 10–12). New York: Joint Council on Economic Education, 1973, 68 pp.

Women on Words and Images. Doctor, Lawyer, Indian Chief. Princeton, NJ: Women on Words and Images, P.O. Box 2163, Princeton, NJ 08540, 1976.

Zeriros, Astaire and Marylee Wiley. Africa in Social Studies Textbooks. Wisconsin Department of Public Instruction, 126 Langdon Street, Madison, Wisconsin 53702, 1978, 34 pp.

Social Studies: Articles

Abramowitz, Jack. "Textbooks and Negro History," Social Education, March, 1969, 33, 306–309.

Alexander, Albert, "Does the American History Textbook Still Wear a Gray Flannel Cover?" Social Education, March, 1969, 33, 300–305.

Alilunas, Leo J. "The Image of Public Schools in Roman Catholic American History Textbooks," History of Education Quarterly, September 3, 1963, 3, 159–165.

Allen, Van A. "An Analysis of Textbooks Relative to the Treatment of Black Americans," Journal of Negro Education, Winter, 1971, 6.

Anyon, Jean. "Elementary Social Studies

Textbooks and Legitimating Knowledge," *Theory and Research in Social Education*, April 1979, *6*, 40–55.

Anyon, Jean. "Ideology and United States History Textbooks," *Harvard Education Review*, August, 1979, *9*, 361–386.

"Asian Americans in Children's Books," *Interracial Books for Children Bulletin*, 1976, *7*, 2–3, 40.

Banks, James A. "A Content Analysis of the Black American in Textbooks," *Social Education*, December, 1969, *33*, 954–957.

Barger, Harold M. "Demythologizing the Textbook President: Teaching About the President After Watergate," *Theory and Research in Social Education*, August, 1976, *4*, 1, 51–66.

Benjamin, James M. "What Have We Done to Social Studies?" *Social Education*, February, 1975, *39*, 2, 88–90.

Billington, R. A. "History Is a Dangerous Subject," *Saturday Review*, January 15, 1966, *49*, 59–61, 80–81.

Blythe, Irene T. "The Textbooks and the New Discoveries, Emphasis and Viewpoints in American History," *Historical Outlook*, *23*, 395–402.

Brazziel, William F. "Negro History in Public Schools: Trends and Prospects," *Negro History Bulletin*, November, 1965, *28*, 36–38.

Britton, Gwyneth E. "Sex Stereotyping and Career Roles," *Journal of Reading*, November, 1973, *17*, 2, 140–148.

Burns, Roger and Omer J. Rupiper. "Trends in School Psychology as Demonstrated by Content Analysis of School Psychology Textbooks," *Psychology in the Schools*, July, 1977, *14*, 3, 332–339.

Buys, Christian J. "Freud in Introductory Psychology Texts," *Teaching of Psychology*, December, 1976, *3*, 4, 160–167.

Chapman, Anne. "Women in the History Curriculum," *Social Studies*, May–June, 1978, *69*, 3, 117–121.

Cunningham, George E. "Derogatory Image of the Negro and Negro History," *Negro History Bulletin*, March, 1965, *28*, 26–27.

Davis, Lucian. "Current Controversy: Minorities in American History Textbooks," *Journal of Secondary Education*, November, 1966, *41*, 291–294.

Dolgin, Ann B. "Ethnic Textbooks and Cross-cultural Awareness," *Trends in Social Education*, Fall, 1977, *24*, 1, 11–13.

Dunne, Eugene E. and Luciano L'Abate. "The Family Taboo in Psychology Textbooks," *Teaching of Psychology*, October, 1978, *5*, 3, 115–117.

Dunne, Eugene L. and Luciano L'Abate. "The Family Taboo in Psychology Textbooks," *Teaching of Psychology*, November, 1978, *5*, 186–188.

Edelman, Murray. "American Politics Texts and Political Reality," *Teaching Political Science*, April, 1977, *4*, 3, 265–268.

EPIE Report, "Secondary School Social Studies: Analysis of 31 Textbook Programs," November/December, 1975, #71, 1–96.

Fetsko, William. "Textbooks and the New Social Studies," *Social Studies*, March–April, 1979, *70*, 2, 51–55.

Fitch, Robert M. and James S. VanNess. "The Historian's Contribution?" *Social Education*, November, 1966, *30*, 502–506.

FitzGerald, Frances, "History Textbooks (Parts I, II, III)," *The New Yorker*, February 26, 1979, March 5, 1979, and March 12, 1979, vol. LV. (Also published in book form.)

Gaines, John S. "Treatment of Mexican-American History in High School Textbooks," *Civil Rights Digest*, October, 1972, *5*, 35–40.

Garcia, Jesus. "Ethnic Group Images in History Texts," *Social Studies*, November–December, 1977, *68*, 6, 241–244.

Garcia, Jesus. "Ethnicity in Textbooks," *Educational Digest*, April, 1978, *43*, 27–30.

Garcia, Jesus. "Ethnicity in Textbooks," *Lutheran Education*, January–February, 1977, *113*, 152–161.

Garcia, Jesus. "From Bloody Savages to Heroic Chiefs: California Adopted 8th Grade Textbooks," *Journal of American Indian Education*, January, 1979, *17*, 15–19.

Garcia, Jesus and C. S. Woodrick. "Treatment of White and Non-White Women in U.S. Textbooks," *Clearinghouse*, Summer, 1979, *53*, 17–22.

Gibson, Emily Fuller. "The Three D's: Distortion, Deletion, Denial," *Social Education*, April, 1969, *33*, 405–409.

Glancy, Barbara. "The Beautiful People in Children's Books," *Childhood Education*, April, 1970, *46*, 365–370.

Golden, Loretta. "The Treatment of Minority Groups in Primary Social Studies Textbooks," *Interracial Review*, September, 1966, *39*, 150–154.

Griswold, William J. "Images of the Middle East," *Rocky Mountain Social Studies Journal*, January, 1974, *11*, 1, 25–36.

Groff, Patrick. "The Abolitionist Movement in High School Texts," *Journal of Negro History*, 1963, *32*, 45.

Hall, S. J. "What Do Textbooks Teach Our Children About Africa?" *Interracial Books for Children Bulletin*, 1978, *9*, 3, 3–10.

Hanvey, Robert. "Augury for the Social Studies," *School Review*, 1961, *68*, 11–24.

Harris, Nelson H. "The Treatment of Negroes in Books and Media Designed for the Elementary School," *Social Education*, April, 1969, *33*, 434–437.

Hawkins, Michael L. "Map and Globe Skills in Elementary School Textbooks," *Journal of Geography*, December, 1977, *76*, 7, 261–265.

Hawkins, Michael L. "Pictorial Bias in Elementary Social Studies Textbooks," *Negro Educational Review*, July–October, 1978, *29*, 3–4, 220–224.

Henry, Jeannette. "Our Inaccurate Textbooks," *The Indian Historian*, December 1967, *1*.

Henry, Jules, "Education for Stupidity," *The New York Review*, May 9, 1968, *13*, 30–36.

Henry, Jules. "Reading for What?" *Teachers College Record*, October, 1963, *65*, 35–49.

Hirschfelder, Arlene B. "The Treatment of Iroquois Indians in Selected American History Textbooks," *Indian Historian*, Fall, 1975, *8*, 2, 31–39.

Hoffman, Abraham. "Textbooks, Mexican Americans, and Twentieth-Century American History," *Teaching History: A Journal of Methods*, Fall, 1978, *3*, 2, 65–72.

Houseman, Gerald L. "The State of the State Texts: A Review Essay," *Indiana Social Studies Quarterly*, Winter, 1977–78, *30*, 3, 20–25.

Howard, Ted. "The First American Revolution: Reality Revived," *Media and Methods*, November, 1975, *12*, 3, 20–24, 64.

Hurst, Joe B. "Political Pablum: Democratic Role Models in Children's Picture Books," *Theory and Research in Social Education*, Fall, 1979, *VII*, 1–19.

Jackson, Richard H. "The Persistence of Outmoded Ideas in High School Geography Texts," *Journal of Geography*, October, 1976, *75*, 7, 399–408.

Janis, Juel. "Educating for Social Stupidity: History, Government and Sociology Textbooks." In Jean Dresden Grambs and John C. Carr (eds.), *Black Image: Education Copes with Color*. Dubuque, Iowa: William C. Brown, 1972.

Joyce, William W. "Minorities in Primary-Grade Social Studies Textbooks: A Progress Report," *Social Education*, March, 1973, vol. 37, pp. 218–233.

Katz, William A. "Minorities in American History Textbooks," *Equal Opportunity Review*, The National Center for Research and Information on Equal Opportunity, The Institute for Urban and Minority Education. New York: Teachers College, Columbia University, June, 1973, 1–4.

Kelly, James R. "Sociology Versus Religion: The Case of the 1973 Sociology Texts," *Teaching Sociology*, July, 1977, *4*, 4, 357–370.

Kirkness, Verna J. "Prejudice about Indians in Textbooks," *Journal of Reading*, April, 1977, *20*, 7, 595–600.

Kownslar, Allan O. "What Should Be Done to the Social Studies: A Response to 'What Have We Done to Social Studies?'" *Social Education*, February, 1975, *39*, 2, 89–91.

Krug, Mark M. "Distant Cousins: A Comparative Study of Selected History Textbooks in England and in the United States," *School Review*, Winter, 1963, *71*, 425–441.

Krug, Mark M. "Freedom and Racial Equality: A Study of 'Revised' High School History Texts," *School Review*, May, 1970, *78*, 297–344.

Krug, Mark M. "On Rewriting the Story of Reconstruction in the United States History Textbooks," *The Journal of Negro History*, April, 1961, *46*, 133–153.

Krug, Mark M. "Safe Textbooks and Citizenship Education," *School Review*, 1960, *68*, 463–480.

Kwitman, Lois. "The Treatment of Population in Secondary School Social Studies Textbooks," *Journal of Environmental Education*, 1974, *5*, 4, 37–41.

Landes, David. "The Treatment of Population in History Textbooks," *Daedalus*, Spring, 1968, *97*, 363–384.

Lenarcic, R. J. "Telling It Like It Wasn't—History and the American Indian," *Community College Social Science Journal*, 1976–77, *1*, 1, 9–11, 14.

Main, Robert S. "The Treatment of Economic Issues in High School Government, Sociology, U.S. History and World History Texts," *Journal of Economic Education*, Spring, 1978, *9*, 2, 115–118.

Mallam, R. Clark. "Academic Treatment of the Indian in Public School Texts and Literature," *Journal of American Indian Education*, October, 1973, *13*, 1, 14–19.

Manicas, Peter. "The Social Studies, Philosophy and Politics," *Social Studies*, November–December, 1978, *69*, 6, 244–248.

Margolis, Richard J. "The Well-Tempered Textbook," *Education Digest*, December, 1965, *31*, 24–27.

Martin, David S. "Ethnocentrism Toward Foreign Cultures in Elementary Social Studies," *Elementary School Journal*, March, 1975.

Mayer, Martin. "The Trouble with Textbooks," *Harper's*, July, 1962, *205*, 65–71.

McAulay, J. D. "Evaluation of Textbook Content on Southeast Asia," *Clearing House*, November, 1978, *52*, 3, 105–106.

McPherson, James. "The 'Saga' of Slavery: Setting the Textbooks Straight," *Changing Education*, Winter, 1967, *2*, 26–33.

Meyer, Howard N. "Overcoming the Whiteman's History," *Massachusetts Review*, 1966, *7*, 569–578.

Moore, Robert B. "Sexism in Textbooks," *Social Studies*, May–June, 1978, *69*, 112–116.

Morgan, Edmund S. "An Anglo-American Contribution to Historical Misunderstanding,"

Social Education, November, 1966, *30*, 499–502.

Myers, Charles B. and Thomas B. Stitely. "Environment-Related Topics in Social Studies Student Materials: A Survey," *Peabody Journal of Education*, October, 1973, *51*, 1, 47–52.

Noah, Harold J., Carl E. Prince, and C. Russell Riggs. "History in High School Textbooks: A Note," *School Review*, 1962, *70*, 415–436.

O'Donnel, Richard W. "Sex Bias in Primary Social Studies Textbooks," *Educational Leadership*, November, 1973, *31*, 137–141.

Oliver, James K. and James A. Nathan. "Political Change and Political Choice: A Review of Some Introductory American Government Texts," *Teaching Political Science*, July, 1976, *3*, 4, 445–460.

O'Neill, James B. and Richard Newton. "Economics—Forgotten Social Science in Today's U.S. History Books," *High School Journal*, March, 1975, *58*, 274–283.

Palmer, John R. "History Textbooks and Social Change," *Social Education*, March, 1961, *25*, 135–136.

Parenti, Michael. "The Purpose of American Government Textbooks: A Response to Oliver and Nathan," *Teaching Political Science*, April, 1977, *4*, 3, 257–262.

Pasternack, Elliot L. "American History Textbooks: The Case of the Missing Minority," *Community College Social Science Quarterly*, Summer—Fall, 1975, *5*, 4–6, 1, 105–107, 138.

Peters, Marie Ferguson. "The Black Family—Perpetuating the Myths: An Analysis of Family Sociology Textbook Treatment of Black Families," *Family Coordinator*, October, 1974, *23*, 4, 349–356.

Polos, N. C. "Textbooks and the Invisible Man," *Educational Forum*, May, 1967, *31*, 477–480.

Qureshi, M. Y. and Michael R. Zulli. "A Content Analysis of Introductory Psychology Textbooks," *Teaching of Psychology*, April, 1975, *2*, 2, 60–65.

Qureshi, M. Y. and Paul R. Sackett. "An Updated Content Analysis of Introductory Psychology Textbooks," *Teaching of Psychology*, February, 1977, *4*, 1, 25–30.

Rader, Benjamin G. "Jacksonian Democracy: Myth or Reality?" *Social Studies*, January, 1974, *65*, 1, 17–21.

Rosen, Philip. "American History Textbooks and Immigrants: Time for a Fair Shake," *Social Studies Journal*, Spring, 1974, *3*, 1, 16–21.

Schwartz, Lita Linzer and Natalie Isser. "Forgotten Minorities, Self-Concept, and the Schools," *Social Studies*, September–October, 1978, *69*, 5, 187–190.

Seller, Maxine, and Andrew Trusz. "High School Textbooks and the American Revolution," *History Teacher*, August, 1976, *9*, 4, 535–555.

Shaver, James P. "Diversity, Violence, and Religion: Textbooks in a Pluralistic Society," *School Review*, August, 1967, *75*, 311–327.

Shaver, James P. "Political and Economic Socialization in Elementary School Social Studies Textbooks: A Reaction," *Theory and Research in Social Education*, Spring, 1979, *7*, 43–48.

Shaver, James P. "Reflective Thinking. Values and Social Studies Textbooks," *School Review*, Autumn, 1965, *73*, 226, 676.

Shrag, Peter. "The Emasculated Voice of the Textbook," *Saturday Review*, January 21, 1967, *50*, 74.

Sloan, Irving. "Balance and Imbalance: New History Texts and the Negro," *Changing Education*, Fall, 1966, *1*, 14–19.

Sohn, David. "The Rationale for the Practice of Randomly Assigning Subjects to Groups: Its Treatment in Textbooks in Experimental Psychology, and Some Suggestions," *Teaching of Psychology*, April, 1977, *4*, 2, 87–88.

Stampp, Kenneth, et al. "The Negro in American History Textbooks," *Integrated Education*, October–November, 1964, *2*, 9–25.

Stewart, Charles E. "Correcting the Image of Negroes in Textbooks," *Negro History Bulletin*, November, 1964, *28*, 29–30.

Taxel, Joel. "Justice and Cultural Conflict: Racism, Sexism and Instructional Materials," *Interchange: A Journal of Education Studies*, 1979, *9*, 56–84.

Textbook Committee of the Committee on Economic Education of the American Economic Association. "Economics in the Schools," *American Economic Review*, 1963 *53*, 1–27 (part 2 supplement).

"The Writing and Teaching of American History in Textbooks," *AHA Newsletter*, April, 1969, *4*, 7–10.

Trecker, Janice Law. "Women in U.S. History Textbooks," *Social Education*, March, 1971, *35*, 249–260.

Trezise, Robert L. "The Black American in American History Textbooks," *Social Studies*, April, 1969, *60*, 164–167.

Triebwasser, Marc A. "Politics, Economics, and American Government Texts," *Teaching Political Science*, April, 1977, *4*, 3, 269–278.

Turetsky, F. "Treatment of Black Americans in Primary Grade Textbooks Used in New York City Elementary Schools," *Graduate Research Education*, Spring, 1975, *8*, 98–144.

Voelker, Alan M. and Christine L. Kolb. "The

Presence of Environmental Resource Management Themes in Selected Problems-of-Democracy Textbooks," *Journal of Environmental Education,* Winter, 1973, *5,* 2, 52–60.

Vogel, Virgil J. "The Indian in American History Textbooks," *Integrated Education,* May–June, 1968, *33,* 16–22.

Vogel, Virgil J. "The Indian in American History," *Social Education,* February, 1969, *33,* 200–203.

Weitzman, Lenore J. and Diane Rizzo, "Sex Bias in Textbooks," *Today's Education,* January–February, 1975, *64,* 49–52.

Witter, Janet (ed.). "Bias in the Textbooks: A Symposium," Oregon ASCD *Curriculum Bulletin.* Entire Issue November, 1977, *31,* 337, 32.

Wood, Herbert J. "The Far East in World History," *Social Education,* April, 1951, *15,* 155–159.

Wright, Vicki. "Hidden Messages: Expressions of Prejudice," *Interchange,* 1976–1977, *7,* 2, 54–62.

Yee, Albert H. "Myopic Perceptions and Textbooks: Chinese Americans' Search for Identity," *Journal of Social Issues,* 1973, *29,* 2, 99–114.

Zimmerman, Roger. "Social Studies Textbooks Still Neglect Racial Minorities and Women and Short Change Children," *Negro Educational Review,* April–July, 1975, *26,* 2–3, 116–123.

Zuercher, Roger. "The Treatment of Asian Minorities in American History Textbooks," *The Indiana Social Studies Quarterly,* Autumn, 1969, *22,* 19–27.

Cross-Cultural Analysis

Anleiman, M. W. "Values Expressed in Egyptian Children's Readers," *Cross-Cultural Psychology,* Spring, 1977, *8,* 347–355.

Aoki, Ted T. "Curriculum Approaches to Canadian Ethnic Histories in the Context of Citizenship Education," *History and Social Science Teacher,* Winter, 1978, *13,* 2, 95–99.

Bachman, Siegfried. "Comparative Textbook Analysis," *Education and Culture,* Autumn, 1976, *31,* 33–37.

Barendsen, Robert D. "America's Revolution As Others See It," *American Education,* June, 1976, *12,* 5, 28–29.

Cary, Charles D. "Natural Themes in Soviet School History Textbooks," *Computers and the Humanities,* November/December, 1976, *10,* 6, 313–323.

Cary, Charles D. "Patterns of Emphasis upon Marxist-Leninist Ideology: A Computer Content Analysis of Soviet School History, Geography, and Social Science Textbooks," *Comparative Education Review,* February, 1976, *20,* 1, 11–29.

Dance, E. H. "To Each His Own Truth," *Times Educational Supplement,* London, November 29, 1974, 3105, 21.

Darten, F. J. Harvey. *Children's Books in England: Five Centuries of Social Life.* Cambridge: Cambridge University Press, 1960.

d'Heurle, Adma, et al. "World View of Folktales: A Comparative Study," *Elementary School Journal,* November, 1975, *76,* 2, 75–89.

Dominy, Mildred M. "A Comparison: Textbooks, Domestic and Foreign," *Arithmetic Teacher,* November, 1963, *10,* 428–434.

Grund-Slepack, Donna and Marvin J. Berlowitz. "Sex Role Stereotyping in East German versus U.S. Textbooks," *Reading Teacher,* December, 1977, *31,* 3, 275–279.

Jennison, Earl W., Jr. "The Neglected 'Ethnics' in Russian History Surveys," *History Teacher,* May, 1975, *8,* 3, 437–451.

Lorimer, Rowland, et al. "Language Arts Reading Series," *Interchange,* 1977–78, *8,* 4, 64–77.

Lupul, M. R. "The Portrayal of Canada's 'Other' Peoples in Senior High School History and Social Studies Textbooks in Alberta, 1905 to the Present," *Alberta Journal of Educational Research,* March, 1976, *22,* 1, 1–33.

Slevin, Carl. "Ruling Types," *Times Educational Supplement,* London, October 11, 1974, 3098, 27.

Votey, E. Scott. "Political Attitudes Reflected in Soviet Elementary Textbooks," *Social Education,* March, 1978, *42,* 3, 228–230.

Weiner, Gaby. "Education and the Sex Discrimination Act," *Educational Research,* June, 1978, *20,* 3, 163–173, (Great Britain).

Wiberg, J. Lawrence and Gaston E. Blom, "A Cross-National Study of Attitude Content in Reading Primers," *International Journal of Psychology,* November 2, 1970, *5,* 109–122.

Zak, Itai and Shlomit Kaufman. "Sex Stereotypes in Israeli Primers: A Content Analysis Approach," *Studies in Education Evaluation,* Spring, 1977, *3,* 27–77.

Elementary School Reading Texts

Blom, Gaston E., Richard R. Waite, and Sarah F. Zimet, "Ethnic Integration and Urbanization of a First Grade Reading Textbook: A Research Study," *Psychology in the Schools,* April, 1967, *4,* 176–184.

Butterfield, Robin A., et al. "Multicultural Analysis of a Popular Basal Reading Series in the International Year of the Child," *Journal of Negro Education,* Summer, 1979, *48,* 3, 382–389.

Cheek, Earl H., Jr., and Martha C. Cheek. "A Realistic Evaluation of Current Basal Readers," *Phi Delta Kappan,* May, 1979, *60,* 9, 682.

Collier, Marilyn. "An Evaluation of Multi-Ethnic Basal Readers," *Elementary English,* February, 1967, *44,* 152–157.

duCharms, Richard and Gerald H. Moeler. "Values Expressed in American Children's Readers," *Journal of Abnormal and Social Psychology,* 1962, *64,* 136–142.

Fishman, Anne Stevens. "A Criticism of Sexism in Elementary Readers," *Reading Teacher,* February, 1976, *29,* 5, 443–446.

Graebner, D.B. "A Decade of Sexism in Readers," *The Reading Teacher,* February, 1972, *26,* 52–58.

Graney, Marshall. "Role Models in Children's Readers," *School Review,* February, 1977, *85,* 2, 247–263.

Jacklin, Carol N. and Harriet N. Mischell. "As the Twig Is Bent: Sex Role Stereotyping in the Early Readers," *The School Psychology Digest,* Summer, 1973, *2,* 30–38.

Kidd, Virginia. " 'Now You See,' Said Mark," *New York Review,* September 3, 1970, *15,* 35–36.

Kingston, A.J. and T. Lovelace. "Sexism and Reading: A Critical Review of the Literature," *Reading Quarterly,* 1977–78, *13,* 1, 133–161.

Kyle, Diane W. "Changes in Basal Reader Content: Has Anyone Been Listening?" *Elementary School Journal,* May, 1978, *78,* 5, 304–312.

Luker, William A., et al. "Elementary School Basal Readers and Work Mode Bias," *Journal of Economic Education,* Spring, 1974, *5,* 2, 92–96.

"Many Faces of Change: Happiness vs. Conflict in Current Basal Readers," *EPIEgram: Materials,* May, 1979, 7, 2–3.

Marten, Laurel A. and Margaret W. Matlin. "Does Sexism in Elementary Readers Still Exist?" *Reading Teacher,* May, 1976, *29,* 8, 764–767.

McCloud, Barbara K., et al. "Content Analysis of Basal Reading Texts for Normal and Retarded Children," *Journal of Special Education* Fall, 1976, *10,* 3, 259–264.

McCutcheon, Gail, et al. "Characters in Basal Readers: Does 'Equal' Now Mean 'Same'?" *Reading Teacher,* January, 1979, *32,* 438–441.

Schnell, T. R. and J. Sweeney. "Sex Role Bias in Basal Readers," *Elementary English,* 1975, *52,* 737–742.

Sexism and Racism in Popular Basal Readers 1964–1976. Council on Interracial Books for Children, 1841 Broadway, NY 10023, 1976, 43 pp.

Smith, Patricia K. "Personality and Behavior Traits in Basal Readers," *Reading Horizons,* Summer, 1977, *17,* 4, 275–279.

Stefflre, Buford. "Run Mama Run: Women Workers in Elementary Readers," *Vocational Guidance Quarterly,* December, 1969, *18,* 99–102.

Taylor, Marjorie E. "Sex-Role Stereotypes in Children's Readers," *Elementary English,* October, 1973, *50,* 7, 1045–1047.

Waite, Richard R. "Further Attempts to Integrate and Urbanize First Grade Textbooks: A Research Study," *Journal of Negro Education,* Winter, 1968, *37,* 62–69.

Wargny, Frank O. "The Good Life in Modern Readers," *Reading Teacher,* November, 1963, *17,* 88–93.

Women on Words and Images. *Dick and Jane as Victims: Sex Stereotyping in Children's Readers.* Princeton, New Jersey: Women on Words and Images, 1972.

Zimet, Sara F. "American Elementary Reading Textbooks: A Sociological Review," *Teachers College Record,* January, 1969, *70,* 331–340.

Zimet, Sara Goodman (ed.). *What Children Read in School: Critical Analysis of Primary Reading Textbooks.* New York: Grune and Stratton, 1972.

Other School Textbooks

Babikian, Elijah. "An Aberrated Image of Science in Elementary School Science Textbooks," *School Science and Mathematics,* May–June, 1975, *75,* 5, 457–460.

Boschmann, Hugo, et al. "Six State Adopted Biology Textbooks: Do They Raise Bioethical Issues?" *Hoosier Science Teacher,* September, 1978, *4,* 1, 13–20.

Hutton, Sandra S. "Sex-Role Illustrations in Junior High School Home Economics Textbooks," *Journal of Home Economics,* March, 1976, *68,* 2, 27–30.

Jay, Winifred T. and Clarence W. Schminke. "Sex Bias in Elementary Mathematics Texts," *The Arithmetic Teacher,* 1975, *22.*

Kent, Gyann and Ronald D. Simpson. "An Analysis of Sex-Related Topics in High School Biology," *American Biology Teacher,* January, 1976, *38,* 1, 34–39.

LeClercq, Frederic S. "The Constitution and Creationism," *American Biology Teacher,* March, 1974, *36,* 3, 139–145.

Lynch, James J. and Bertrand Evans. *High School English Textbooks: A Critical Examination.* Boston: Atlantic–Little, Brown, 1965.

McLean, Gary N., et al. "Sexism in General Business Texts," *Journal of Business Education,* February, 1978, *53,* 5, 215–217.

Moore, John A. "Creationism in California," *Daedalus,* Summer, 1974, *103,* 173–189.

Newell, Norman D. "Evolution Under Attack," *Natural History*, April, 1974, *LXXXIII*, 32–39.

Shirreffs, Janet H. "Sex Role Stereotyping in Elementary School Health Education Textbooks," *Journal of School Health*, 1975, *XLV*, 9, 5.

Steel, Barbara. "Sexism in Math Texts," *Edcentric*, Spring-Summer, 1977, *40–41*, 17–19.

Taylor, J. "Sexist Bias in Physics Textbooks," *Physics Education*, July, 1979, *14*, 5, 277–280.

Wade, Nicholas. "Creationists and Evolutionists: Confrontation in California," *Science*, November 17, 1972, *178*, 724–729.

Weis, Susan F. "Examinations of Home Economics Textbooks for Sex Bias," *Home Economics Research Journal*, January, 1979, 7, 3, 147–162.

Yost, Michael. "Similarity of Science Textbooks: A Content Analysis," *Journal of Research in Science Teaching*, 1973, *10*, 4, 317–322.

Children's Literature

Abel, Midge. "American Indian Life as Portrayed in Children's Literature," *Elementary English*, February, 1973, *50*, 202–208.

Ansello, Edward F. "Ageism in Picture Books: Part I—How Older People Are Stereotyped: Part II—"The Rocking Chair Syndrome in Action," *Bulletin, Interracial Books for Children*, November 6, 1976, 7, 3–10.

Ansello, E. F. "Literature, Mentality and Aging." In Harvey L. Sterns, et al. (eds.), *Gerontology in Higher Education: Developing Institutional and Community Strength*. Belmont, CA: Wadsworth Publishing Co., 1980, pp. 116–127.

Ansello, E. F. "Old Age and Literature: An Overview," *Educational Gerontology*, 1977, *2* (3) 211–218.

Ansello, E. F. "Age and Ageism in Children's First Literature," *Educational Gerontology*, 1977, *2* (3) 255–274.

Ansello, E. F. "Ageism—The Subtle Stereotype," *Childhood Education*, 1978, *54* (3), 118–122.

Barnum, Phyllis W. "Discrimination Against the Aged in Young Children's Literature," *The Elementary School Journal*, March, 1977, *77*, 301–306.

Baxter, Katherine B. "Combating the Influence of Black Stereotypes in Children's Books," *Reading Teacher*, March, 1974, *27*, 6, 540–544.

Black, Hillel. "What Our Children Read," *Saturday Evening Post*, October 7, 1967, *240*, 27–29.

Blatt, Gloria T. "Mexican-Americans in Children's Literature," *Elementary English*, April, 1968, *45*, 446–451.

Bovyer, George G. "Stories and Children's Concepts of Sportsmanship in the Fourth, Fifth, and Sixth Grades," *Elementary English*, December, 1962, *39*, 762–765.

Bracken, Jeanne and Sharon Wigutoff. "Sugar and Spice: That's What Children's Books Are Still Made Of," *Women Studies Newsletter*, Summer, 1977, *V*, 3. The Feminist Press, Box 334, Old Westbury, NY 11568.

Byler, Mary G. "The Image of American Indians Projected by Non-Indian Writers," *Library Journal*, February 15, 1974, *99*, 546–549.

Crosby, Faye, et al., "Sexism and Racism in Pre-School Books: Temporal Trends," *Journal Supplement Abstract Service*, American Psychological Association, 1200 17th Street, NW, Washington, D.C. 20034, 1977.

Daniels, Leona. "The 34th Man: How Well Is Jewish Minority Culture Represented in Children's Fiction?" In Lillian Gerhardt (ed.), *Issues in Children's Book Selection*, New York: Bowker, 1973, 90–101.

Davis, Mavis W. "Black Images in Children's Literature," *Library Journal*, January, 1972.

Epstein, Jason. "Good Bunnies Always Obey: Books for American Children," *Commentary*, February, 1963, *2*, 112–122.

Falkenhagen, Maria, Carole Johnson, and Michael A. Balasa. "The Treatment of Native Americans in Recent Children's Literature," *Integrated Education*, July-October, 1973, *XI*, 58–59.

Falkenhagen, Maria and Inga K. Kelly, "The Native American in Juvenile Fiction: Teacher Perception of Stereotypes," *Journal of American Indian Education*, January 1974, *13*, 2, 9–13.

Fisher, Laura. "All Chiefs, No Indians: What Children's Books Say About American Indians," *Elementary English*, February, 1974, *51*, 2, 185–189.

Gast, E. "Minority Americans in Children's Literature," *Elementary English*, January, 1967, *44*, 12–23.

Glancy, Barbara J. "Why Good Interracial Books Are Hard to Find." In Jean Dresden Grambs and John C. Carr (eds.), *Black Image: Education Copes with Color*. Dubuque, Iowa: William C. Brown, 1972, 44–47.

Hillman, Judith S. "An Analysis of Male and Female Roles in Two Periods in Children's Literature," *The Journal of Educational Research*, October, 1974, *68*, 84–89.

Homze, Alma. "Interpersonal Relations in Children's Literature, 1920–1950," *Elementary English*, January, 1966, *43*, 26–27.

Jones, James P. "Negro Stereotypes in Children's Literature: The Case of Nancy Drew," *Journal of Negro Education*, Winter, 1971, *40*, 122–132.

Kelty, Jean Mc. "The Cult of Kill in Adolescent Fiction," *English Journal*, February, 1975, *64*, 56–61.

Key, Mary Ritchie. "The Role of Male and Female in Children's Books," *Wilson Library Bulletin*, October, 1971, *46*, 167–176.

Larrick, Nancy. "The All-White World of Children's Books," *Saturday Review*, September 11, 1965, *48*, 63–66.

Lieberman, Marcia. "Some Day My Prince Will Come: Female Acculturation Through the Fairy Tale," *College English*, December, 1972, *34*, 383–395.

Lowry, Heath W. "A Review of Five Recent Content Analyses of Related Sociological Factors in Children's Literature," *Elementary English*, October, 1969, *46*, 736–740.

Lukenbill, W. Bernard. "Fathers in Adolescent Novels: Some Implications in Sex Role Reinterpretation," *Library Journal*, February, 1974, *4*, 536–540.

MacCann, Donnarae and Gloria Woodard (eds.). *The Black American in Books for Children.* Metuchen, N.J.: Scarecrow Press, 1972.

Mandel, R. L. "Children's Books; Mirrors of Social Development," *Elementary School Journal*, January, 1964, *65*, 190–199.

McClelland, David C. "Values in Popular Literature for Children," *Childhood Education*, November, 1963, *40*, 135–138.

Moore, Vardine. "The Feminine Role in Children's Books," *Educational Horizons*, Winter 1973–74, *52*, 2, 93–94.

Muller, Al. "Thirty Popular Adolescent Novels: A Content Analysis," *English Journal*, September, 1974, *63*, 97–99.

Nilsen, Alleen Pace. "Sexism in Children's Books and Elementary Classroom Materials." In Alleen Pace Nilsen, et al. (eds.), *Sexism and Language.* Urbana, Ill.: National Council of Teachers of English, 1977, 161–179.

Preer, Bette B. "Guidance in Democratic Living Through Juvenile Fiction," *Wilson Library Bulletin*, May, 1948, *22*, 679–681.

Pyle, Wilma J. "Sexism in Children's Literature," *Theory Into Practice*, April, 1976, *15*, 2, 116–119.

Sadker, Myra P. and David M. Sadker. *Now Upon a Time: A Contemporary View of Children's Literature.* New York: Harper and Row, 1977.

Scott, K. P. and S. Feldman-Summers. "Children's Reactions to Textbook Stories in Which Females Are Portrayed in Traditionally Male Roles," *Journal of Educational Psychology*, July, 1979, *71*, 396–402.

Shepard, J. P. "The Treatment of Characters in Popular Children's Fiction," *Elementary English*, November, 1962, *39*, 672–676.

Siegel, Selma R. "Heroines in Recent Children's Fiction: an Analysis," *Elementary English*, October, 1973, *50*, 1039–1044.

Sledd, James. "Essay Review: As in Itself It Really Is," *School Review*, Autumn, 1966, *74*, 341–352.

Stensland, Anna Lee. *Literature By and About the American Indian.* Urbana, Illinois: National Council of Teachers of English, 1973.

Stoer, M. W. "A Second Look: The Treatment of Characters in Popular Children's Fiction," *Elementary English*, February, 1963, *40*, 172–173.

Stoodt, Barbara D. and Ignizio, Sandra. "The American Indian in Children's Literature," *Language Arts*, January, 1976, *53*, 1, 17–19.

Storey, Denise G. "Gray Power, An Endangered Species: Ageism as Portrayed in Children's Books," *Social Education*, October, 1977, *43*, 528–531.

Tate, Janice M. "Sexual Bias in Science Fiction for Children," *Elementary English*, October, 1973, *50*, 1061–1064.

Tibbetts, Sylvia L. "What's So Funny? Humor in Children's Literature," *California Journal of Educational Research*, January, 1973, *24*, 42–46.

Tully, Deborah S. "Nature Stories—Unrealistic Fiction," *Elementary English*, March, 1974, *51*, 348–352.

Walton, Jeanne. "The American Negro in Children's Literature," *Eliot-Pearson School News*, Tufts University, February, 1964.

Weitzman, Lenore J., et al. "Sex-Role Socialization in Picture Books for Pre-School Children," *American Journal of Sociology*, May, 1972, *77*, 1125–1149.

Wiberg, John L. and Marion Trost. "A Comparison Between the Content of First Grade Primers and the Free Choice of Library Selections Made by First Grade Students," *Elementary English*, October, 1970, *47*, 792–798.

Yawkey, Thomas D. and Margaret L. Yawkey. "An Analysis of Picture Books," *Language Arts*, May, 1976, *53*, 5, 545–548.

Zimet, Sara G. "Little Boy Lost," *Teachers College Record*, September, 1970, *72*, 31–40.

Zwack, Jean. "The Stereotype Family in Children's Literature," *Reading Teacher*, January, 1973, *26*, 389–391.

College Texts and Material for Adults

Bonin, Therese and Judith Muryskens. "French Women in Language Textbooks: Fact or Fiction?" *Contemporary French Civilization*, 1977, *2*, 11, 135–151.

Brazelton, W. Robert. "Samuelson's Principles of Economics in 1948 and 1973," *Journal of Economic Education*, Spring, 1977, *8*, 2, 115–117.

Childress, Alice, et al. "The Negro Woman in American Literature," *Freedomways*, April, 1966, *6*, 9–25.

Coles, Gerald S. "Dick and Jane Grow Up: Ideology in Adult Basic Education Readers," *Urban Education*, April, 1977, *12*, 1, 37–54.

Doolittle, Robert J. "Conflicting Views of Conflict: An Analysis of Basic Speech Communication Textbooks," *Communication Education*, March, 1977, *26*, 2, 121–127.

Dressel, Paula L. and W. Ray Avant. "Aging and College Family Textbooks," *Family Coordinator*, October, 1978, *27*, 4, 427–435.

Findley, W. G. "Treatment of Controversial Issues: A Review of Current Textbooks on Measurement and Evaluation in the Schools," *Educational Horizons*, Fall, 1979, *58*, 59–62.

Gay, Vicky A. "The Image of Women in Psychology Textbooks," *Canadian Psychological Review*, January, 1977, *18*, 46–55.

Goldstein, Michael S. "Drinking and Alcoholism as Presented in College Health Textbooks," *Journal of Drug Education*, Fall, 1975, *5*, 2, 109–123.

Harway, Michelle. "Sex Bias in Counseling Materials," *Journal of College Student Personnel*, January, 1977, *18*, 1, 57–63.

Helgeson, Candace. "The Prisoners of Texts: Male Chauvinism in College Handbooks and Rhetorics," *College English*, December, 1976, *38*, 4, 396–406.

Keukel, William F. "Marriage and the Family in Modern Science Fiction," *Journal of Marriage and the Family*, 1969, *31*, 6–14.

Knoll, Morton, "Administrative Fiction and Credibility," *Public Administration Review*, March, 1965, *25*, 80–84.

Rogers, Katherine M. *The Troublesome Helpmate*. Seattle: University of Washington Press, 1966, Chapter VIII, "The Reason Why," 265–277.

Robinson, Cecil. *With the Ears of Strangers: The Mexican in American Literature*. Tempe, Arizona: The University of Arizona Press, 1963.

Russ, Joanna, "Image of Women in Science Fiction," *Red Clay Reader*, November, 1970, *7*, 6366 Sharon Hills Road, Charlotte, N.C. 28210.

Sadker, Myra P. and David M. Sadker. "Sexism in Teacher Education Texts," *Harvard Education Review*, February, 1980, *40*, 36–46.

Scully, Malcolm G. "Campus Novels Said to Take a Dim View of Teachers and Administrators," *Chronicle of Higher Education*, February 8, 1971, *5*, 1, 8.

Smiley, Sam. *The Drama of Attack: Didactic Plays of the American Depression*. Columbus, Mo.: University of Missouri Press, 1972.

Stern, Rhoda H. "Review Article: Sexism in Foreign Language Textbooks," *Foreign Language Annals*, September, 1976, *9*, 4, 294–299.

Thames, H. Stanley. "Recent International Relations Textbooks: Educational Objectives," *Teaching Political Science*, January, 1979, *6*, 2, 131–149.

Van Valey, Thomas L. "Methods or Not: An Examination of Introductory Texts," *Teaching Sociology*, October, 1975, *3*, 1, 31–32.

Worby, Diana Zacharia. "In Search of a Common Language: Women and Educational Texts," *College English*, September, 1979, *41*, 1, 101–105.

General Studies

Adams, Robert. "Books: The Girl Scout Handbook, Revised Edition," *Esquire*, February, 1964, 38–42.

Arnold, James. "Religious Textbooks . . . Primers in Bigotry." Reprint from *Ave Maria*, Available from American Jewish Committee, New York, 1964.

Belok, Michael V. "The Fictional Academic Woman," *Educational Forum*, January, 1962, 197–203.

Bennett, Lerone, Jr. "The Negro in Textbooks: Reading, 'Riting, and Racism," *Ebony*, March, 1967, *22*, 130–138.

Books for Schools and the Treatment of Minorities, Hearings before the Ad Hoc Subcommittee on De Facto School Segregation of the Committee on Education and Labor, House of Representatives, Eighty-Ninth Congress, Second Session, on Books for Schools and the Treatment of Minorities. Washington, D.C.: U.S. Government Printing Office, 1966, 1–828.

Deegan, Dorothy Yost. *The Stereotype of the Single Woman in American Novels*. New York: King's Crown Press, Columbia University, 1951.

Doherty, Robert E. *Teaching Industrial Relations in High Schools*. Ithaca, New York: State Industrial and Labor Relations, Cornell University, 1964.

Fox, Roy S. "English Methods Books: Bookshelf," *English Education*, October, 1978, *10*, 1, 43–50.

Gay, Geneva. "Impact of Brown on Textbooks," *Crisis*, June-July, 1979, *86*, 240–243.

Grambs, Jean Dresden. "Sex-Stereotypes in Instructional Materials, Literature and Language: A Survey of Research," *Women Studies Abstracts*, Fall, 1972, *1*, 1–4.

Heshusius-Gilsdorf, Louis T. and Dale L. Gilsdorf. "Career Materials," *Personnel and Guidance Journal*, December, 1975, *54*, 4, 207–211.

Holland, Henry M. *Politics Through Literature*. Englewood Cliffs, N.J.: Prentice-Hall, Inc., 1968.

LaNoue, George R. "The National Defense Education Act and 'Secular Subjects,' " *Phi*

Delta Kappan, June, 1962, *43,* 380–388.

Lively, Robert A. *Fiction Fights the Civil War.* Chapel Hill: University of North Carolina, 1957.

Nelkin, Dorothy. "The Science-Textbook Controversies," *Scientific American,* April, 1976, *234,* 4, 33–39.

Olson, Bernhard E. *Faith and Prejudice: Intergroup Problems in Protestant Curricula.* New Haven, Conn.: Yale University Press, 1963.

Rose, Lois and Stephen Rose. *The Shattered Ring: Science Fiction and the Quest for Meaning.* Richmond, Virginia: John Knox, Publisher, 1970.

Sloan, Irving J. "The Selling and the Making of Labor Education in the Schools," *Social Science Record,* February, 1975, *23,* 1, 6–7.

Stewart, Donald C. "Composition Textbooks and the Assault on Tradition," *College Composition and Communication,* May, 1978, *29,* 2, 171–176.

Taylor, Estelle W. "Revised Treatments of Black Americans in Publications after Brown," *Crisis,* June-July, 1979, *86,* 253–257.

U'Ren, Marjorie B. "The Image of Women in Textbooks." In Vivian Gornick and Barbara K. Moran (eds.), *Woman in Sexist Society.* New York: Basic Books, 1971.

Waldo, Dwight. *The Novelist on Organization and Administration: An Inquiry into the Relationship Between Two Worlds.* Berkeley: Institute of Governmental Studies, June, 1968.

Women on Words and Images. *Help Wanted: Sexism in Career Education Materials—How to Detect It and Counteract Its Effects in the Classroom.* Princeton, New Jersey: Women on Words and Images, P.O. Box 2163, Princeton, N.J. 08540, 1975, 51 pp.

Yu, Connie Young. "The 'Others': Asian Americans and Education," *Civil Rights Digest,* February, 1976, *9,* 1, 44–51.

General Comments

Alspektor, Rose Ann and Jeana Wirtenberg (eds.). *Fair Textbooks: A Resource Guide.* Washington, D.C.: United States Commission on Civil Rights, Clearinghouse Publication, December, 1979, *61,* 430 pp.

"Are School Books Really Stereotyped?" *NJEA Review,* October, 1976, *50,* 2, 15.

Bowler, Mike. "Textbook Publishers Try to Please All, But First They Woo the Heart of Texas," *The Reading Teacher,* February, 1978, *31.*

Bragdon, Henry Wilkinson. "Ninth Edition: Adventures with a Textbook," *Independent School,* February, 1978, *37,* 3, 37–41.

Bragdon, Henry W. "Dilemmas of a Textbook Writer," *Social Education,* March, 1969, *33,* 292–298.

Brickman, William W. "Educational Content and the Public Interest," *Intellect,* May/June, 1976, *104,* 2375, 577.

Britton, Gwyneth E. "Danger: State Adopted Texts May Be Hazardous to Our Future," *Reading Teacher,* October, 1975, *29,* 1, 52–58.

Britton, G. E. and M. C. Lumpkin. "For Sale: Subliminal Bias in Textbooks," *Reading Teacher,* October, 1977, *31,* 40–45.

Brody, Celeste M. "Do Instructional Materials Reinforce Sex Stereotyping?" *Educational Leadership,* November, 1973, *31,* 2, 119–122.

Broudy, Eric. "The Trouble with Textbooks," *Teachers College Record,* September, 1975, *77,* 1, 13–34.

Caliguri, Joseph P. "Teacher Bias in the Selection of Social Studies Textbooks," *The Journal of Negro Education,* Fall, 1971, *XL,* 322–329.

Cincotta, Madeleine Strong. "Textbooks and Their Influence on Sex-Role Stereotype Formation," *Babel: Journal of the Australian Federation of Modern Language Teachers' Association,* 1978, *14,* 3, 24–29.

Crane, Barbara. "The 'California Effect' on Textbook Adoptions," *Educational Leadership.* January, 1975, *32,* 4, 283–285.

Cummings, Scott, et al. "Preachers Versus Teachers: Local-Cosmopolitan Conflict over Textbook Censorship in an Appalachian Community," *Rural Sociology,* Spring, 1977, *42,* 1, 7–21.

Deiulio, Anthony M. "Youth Education: A Literary Perspective." In Raymond H. Muessig (ed.), *Youth Education.* Washington, D.C.: Association for Supervision and Curriculum Development, 1968 Yearbook, 58–83.

Dunfee, Maxine (ed.). *Eliminating Ethnic Bias in Instructional Materials: Comment and Bibliography.* Association for Supervision and Curriculum Development, 1707 K Street, N.W., Suite 100, Washington, D.C. 20007, 1974, 58 pp.

Edgerton, Ronald B. "Odyssey of a Book: How a Social Studies Text Comes into Being," *Social Education,* March, 1969, *33,* 279–286.

Elkin, S. M. "Minorities in Textbooks: The Latest Chapter," *Teachers College Record,* March, 1965, *66,* 502–508.

Faigley, Lester I. "What Happened in Kanawha County," *English Journal,* May, 1975, *64,* 4, 7–9.

Foshay, Arthur W. and William W. Burton. "Citizenship as the Aim of the Social Studies," *Theory and Research in Social Education,* December, 1976, *4,* 2, 1–22.

Frank, Libby. "My Weekly Reader Re-Read," *Changing Education,* Spring, 1968, *4,* 60–62.

Gracia, Jesus. "Ethnicity in Textbooks," *Lutheran Education,* January/February, 1978, *113,* 3, 152–161.

Gerushuny, H. Lee. "Sexism in Dictionaries and Texts: Omissions and Commissions." In Aileen Pace Nilsen, et al. (eds.), *Sexism and Language*. Urbana, Ill.: National Council of Teachers of English, 1977, 143–159.

Goldstein, Paul. *Changing the American Schoolbook: Politics, Law, and Technology.* Lexington, Mass.: Lexington Books, 1978.

Graham, Alma. "The Making of a Non-Sexist Dictionary," *MS*, December, 1973, *2*, 12–14.

Grambs, Jean Dresden, and John C. Carr (eds.). *Black Image: Education Copes with Color.* Dubuque, Iowa: Wm. C. Brown, Publisher, 1972.

Hahn, Carole L. "Review of Research on Sex Roles: Implications for Social Studies Research," *Theory and Research in Education*, March, 1978, *6*, 1, 73–99.

Harrison, Linda, and Richard N. Passero. "Sexism in the Language of Elementary School Textbooks," *Science and Children*, January, 1975, *12*, 4, 22–25.

Hester, Nellie. "Textbook Analysis and Community Action," *Elementary English*, May, 1975, *52*, 712–714.

Hodgson, Beverly J. "Sex, Texts, and the First Amendment," *Journal of Law and Education*, April, 1976, *5*, 2, 173–195.

Interracial Books for Children Bulletin. Council on Interracial Books for Children, 1841 Broadway, New York, NY 10023.

Kempton, Patricia C. "Blame the Black Child? His Textbooks Do. . . ," *Journal of Open Education*, Winter, 1974, *2*, 2, 85–93.

Klineberg, Otto. "Life Is Fun in a Smiling, Fair Skinned World," *Saturday Review*, February 16, 1963, *46*, 75.

Kressel, R. H. "The Textbook Family and the Culturally Deprived Pupil," *English Language Teaching Journal*, July, 1974, *28*, 4, 312–315.

Lacy, Dan. "Men's Words; Women's Roles," *Saturday Review*, June 14, 1975, *2*, 19, 25–57.

Luker, William A. and Floyd N. Jenkins. "Work Mode Bias in Elementary Text Materials," *Journal of Industrial Teacher Education*, Fall, 1973, *11*, 1, 16–26.

Massialas, Byron G. *The Politics of Textbook Adoption.* Lexington, Mass.: Lexington Books, 1974.

McConnell, James V. "Confessions of a Textbook Writer," *American Psychologist*, February, 1978, *33*, 3, 159–169.

Monteith, Mary K. "Alternatives to Burning Sexist Textbooks," *Reading Teacher*, December, 1977, *31*, 3, 346–350.

Morrison, Iris, "White Studies," *Forum* for the Discussion of New Trends in Education, April, 1977, *20*, 5–8.

O'Donnell, Holly. "ERIC/RCS Report: Cultural Bias: A Many-Headed Monster," *Elementary English*, February, 1974, *41*, 2, 181–184, 214.

Ohles, John F. "The Literature of Education," *Educational Forum*, May, 1974, *38*, 4, 475–480.

Page, Ann L. and Donald A. Clelland. "The Kanawha County Textbook Controversy: A Study of the Politics of Life Style Concern," *Social Forces*, September, 1978, *57*, 1, 265–281.

Prince, Doris. "Sexism in Instructional Materials," *Thrust for Education Leadership*, October, 1976, *6*, 1, 6–8.

Prosen, Rose Mary. " 'Ethnic Literature'— Who and for Whom: Digressions of a Neo-American Teacher," *College English*, March, 1974, *35*, 6, 659–669.

Reynolds, John C. "Controversy Involving Selection of Science and Humanities Textbooks," *Education*, Spring, 1979, *99*, 3, 350–356.

Roberts, Launey F., Jr. "Ethnocentric Identification: A Survey of the Pictorial Content of Selected Current Elementary School Textbooks," *Negro History Bulletin*, December, 1967, *30*, 6–10.

Rosenberg, Max. "Evaluate Your Textbooks for Racism, Sexism," *Educational Leadership*, November, 1973, *31*, 2, 107–109.

Saario, Terry N., et al. "Sex Role Stereotyping in the Public Schools," *Harvard Educational Review*, August, 1973, *43*, 3, 386–416.

Simms, R. L. "Bias in Textbooks Not Yet Corrected," *Phi Delta Kappan*, November, 1975, *57*, 201–202.

Smith, Shirley. "Crisis in Kanawha County: A Librarian Looks at the Textbook Controversy," *School Library Journal*, January, 1975, *21*, 5, 31–35.

Whelan, John T. "Legislative Process Textbooks and the News Media: A Neglected Link," *Teaching Political Science*, October, 1978, *6*, 1, 89–110.

Taxel, Joel. "Justice and Cultural Conflict: Racism, Sexism, and Instructional Materials," *Interchange: A Journal of Educational Studies*, 1978–79, *9*, 1, 56–84.

Watras, J. "Textbook Dispute in West Virginia: A New Form of Oppression," *Educational Leadership*, October, 1975, *33*, 21–23.

Weston, Louise C. and Sandra L. Stein. "A Content Analysis of Publishers' Guidelines for the Elimination of Sex Role Stereotyping," *Educational Researcher*, March, 1978, *7*, 13–14.

Appendix

An Evaluation Form

The following document is used by textbook committees in the Boulder (Colorado) Public Schools System. It is presented as an example of one type of form that can be used in evaluating textbooks.

BOULDER VALLEY PUBLIC SCHOOLS
DIVISION OF INSTRUCTION

LEARNING MATERIALS SELECTION GUIDE

1. Title of material _____ ISBN # _____

2. Grade level to be used _____

3. Publishing company _____ 4. Copyright date _____

5. Reading level—Appropriateness for the grade level for which it is being considered:

_____ satisfactory   _____ unsatisfactory

scale used: _____
readability level: _____

Comments:

6. Does the content fit course and curriculum objectives?

_____ good   _____ fair   _____ poor

7. Is the content appropriate for the age, maturity, and interests of the students?

_____good   _____ fair   _____ poor

8. General format and organization:

_____ good   _____ fair   _____ poor

Comments:

9. Author: _____ competence in field   _____ unknown in field

Comments:

10. Size of print (where applicable): _____ satisfactory

　　　　　　　　　　　　　　　　　　　　 _____ unsatisfactory

    Comments:

11. Physical features (binding, sound quality, photography quality, etc., as applicable):

        _____ satisfactory　　　_____ unsatisfactory

    Comments:

If items 5 through 11 tend to be unsatisfactory, further examination of this text probably is not indicated; if items 4 through 11 tend to be satisfactory, further examination is recommended.

	Satisfactory	Unsatisfactory	Not Applicable
12. Charts, maps, diagrams, etc. (number) Comments:	_____	_____	_____
13. Charts, maps, diagrams, etc. (clarity) Comments:	_____	_____	_____
14. Pictures (number) Comments:	_____	_____	_____
15. Pictures (clarity) Comments:	_____	_____	_____

16. Cover (attractiveness and appeal) _____ _____ _____

Comments:

17. Size of book (appropriate for age of student) _____ _____ _____

Comments:

	Satisfactory	Unsatisfactory	Not Applicable
18. Table of contents and index	_____	_____	_____

Comments:

| 19. Glossary or definition of terms | _____ | _____ | _____ |

Comments:

| 20. Positive and adequate treatment of minorities | _____ | _____ | _____ |

Comments:

| 21. Positive and adequate treatment of sex roles | _____ | _____ | _____ |

Comments:

22. Type of students at grade level indicated in No. 2 above for which this material seems appropriate:

_____ more able _____ middle _____ less able _____ all _____ none

Comments:

23. Outstanding features of this material:

24. Negative features of this material:

25. General comments:

Using a three-point grading system, with "3" as high and "1" as low, rate this book using the above criteria and your comments as guides.

Basic Text	3	2	1
Supplemental Book	3	2	1
Teacher Reference	3	2	1

_____

Name of Teacher   Grade Level

Revised September 1976

Index